LIVE YOUR LIFE IN TECHNICOLOR.

Marion Collier

A MATTER OF GRACE

by Marion Collier

Dedication

To a Gideon somewhere that left a Bible in a motel room
that shined a light on the path that
became my way to the Big House.

and

To Mattie's memory, to Mattie's miracle, and to Mattie's message.

and

To the Queen Bee of the Zoo, Mary Ann.
To my son, John Clayton Collier, MD.

A Matter of Grace

Contents

Acknowledgments .... *ix*

Foreword .... *xiii*

1   *Life at the Thicket* 15

2   *Life at the Houses of Healing* 24

3   *The Gang Who Lives Here* 33

4   *Mange, Leprosy, and Sin* 42

5   *The Alarm Clock* 52

6   *The Rest of the Gang* 56

7   *We Are Family* 71

8   *Healing from the Inside* 79

9   *The Preacher* 86

10   *Let's Run and Play* 97

11   *Wagons West* 107

12   *The Tale That Wagged the Dog* 122

13   *Stories I Told Mattie* 133

14   *Dog, Pony, and Hog Shows* 143

15   *Look for 'Em, Watch for 'Em, Get 'Em* 153

16   *Confession is Good for the Soul* 159

17   *A Lost Prize* 165

18   *A Trip to the Big House* 172

Acknowledgements

A spark that ignited the desire to tell this story began to smolder deep within my bones. I have shared these feelings with others I trusted. The winds of encouragement began to fan the embers into a raging fire.

Since this path was new for me and a course uncharted, I began to look for guides who had traveled this way before. These guides became the well I drew from, rich in experiences, refreshing in inspiration, and refining in the final phase. I am grateful for the wealth of knowledge, personal experience, and individual sacrifices many made that contributed to the finished work.

The first feedback of my feelings came from my friends at the coffee shop. These early morning sessions are where friends are used as sounding boards. Stirring debates, discussions, and diatribes on any subject imaginable takes place in this setting. Sitting with Roy McDuffie and Don Middleton, Ph.D., I leaned over the table and in a voice near a whisper, I sounded to test the water. Then I cast the bait by saying, "Can you guys keep this under your hats?" Their interest was centered on me as if they were going to be privy to some piece of gossip. After they said nothing and nodded their heads, I said, "What do you think about me writing a book?" I drew strength from the response of these two who also fanned the fire.

Every word of this story was written the old fashioned way, with paper and pen, and with a broken hand, and a broken heart. Someone said I was like a pebble found in a rock quarry that would not find its potential unless it was polished. Many came forward with the elbow grease to provide the polishing.

Since I am technologically illiterate, Jimmy Harper and Roy McDuffie offered their expertise and help. Both are capable and willing; however, since Jimmy already carried a heavy workload, Roy accepted a bigger burden than I think he bargained for. As I think about it, Jimmy owes Roy a bundle. Roy McDuffie has worn the same style haircut for the last seven decades. Even though his flattop has never changed, his life and influence have changed his community, his state, and his world. We are all blessed who can call him our friend. Though older in age he has kept up with the technological age, and his diligence and assistance saw this work to a conclusion. I thank him for helping to gather the wood for the fire.

Two other guides, both authors, pointed in the direction I must travel and offered advice I would need as I moved along. Rev. Oda Wayne "Tuck" Roberts, a polisher by preaching and a writer of experiences, stirred in the embers by placing a gift of his book into my hands. A previous act of polishing me occurred when Brother Roberts gave me a white monogrammed shirt. I knew it was not a hand-me-down because it bore my initials. Putting threads like this with a set of cuff links doesn't change a country boy anymore than putting lipstick on a pig. Someone may make them look better, but they are still a country boy and a pig.

John Guice had recently been down this path, and I had a tremendous amount of confidence that his well was deep and that I could benefit by drawing from it. The Guice family from Winnsboro, Louisiana, is noted to be well versed in writing, grammatical correctness, punctuation, semantics, and syntax. Rebecca Guice, the matriarch of English in Franklin Parish, drilled her students toward language perfection. Early in my preaching days she would come to many services to help me with the errors of my ways, grammar and otherwise. One could say she was polishing the rock. John looked at a small portion of the early manuscript and basically gave this advice. Absolutely, proceed with the book, and tell the story. He said that I was like an amateur athlete with some natural ability but that I needed a lot of polish. He then saved me from the lions when he said it was necessary for me to stay away from my ego. John made it plain that somewhere on the path I must meet someone I trusted, no matter how critical, an editor, that must lead me the rest of the way. I took his advice as I continued the journey.

Did I know a person who fit this description? Absolutely, not one, but two. Jo Ann Williams, English teacher extraordinaire, a marvelous guide who provided the mechanics in helping to polish the language. She promised honesty in evaluating its worth as a work and helped to polish it by covering my ignorance. Mrs. Williams' demands for excellence in her students influenced one who is a "chip off the older block."

Julia Ann Collier Earl, Ph.D., my only sister, who drew from JoAnn's well, brings a fresh taste from her own supply to water the flowers of this story. This time in my life has been most enjoyable as I have reconnected with my sister. We had been separated, only by geography and demands of work, miles apart for 30+ years. Through this project, we have laughed together, we have cried together, we have relived the past together, we have dreamed of the future together, and I have loved every minute of it. She has been the teacher, the umpire, the coach, the referee, the dictator, and the editor whose authority wrecked my ego. The final phase of the trip finds her getting rid of the snakes, pulling up the weeds, scrambling all of the eggs in the book, chunking out the trash, and polishing the rocks. Sound like fun? It was hard work.

A team of teachers who love to give tests agreed to take a test. The eagle eye test and the taste test were handed to each. The eagle eyes began to look for bugs, bits, tidbits, jots, tittles, bears, and elephants. This work was like looking for four-leaf clovers. Then the taste test was given to test the flavor and to see if the recipe needed adjustments of the ingredients. These took and graded the tests: JoAnn Williams, Elaine Netherland, Donna Martin, Debra Park, and Brooke Earl Blevins, Ph.D.

Foreword

T he unfolding of this story began to take place one evening when I was going home from work. Abruptly, the sight arrested my attention. Two poor, pathetic, pitiful, and plagued creatures sat side by side. They were afflicted, abused, afraid, and abandoned on this lonely stretch of road. A trash pile on the side of the road next to the river had now become their home. This story tells how I became involved, a happening that is very hard for me to explain.

The things that took place are above me and beyond me, but very much a part of me. This story is a "Matter of Grace" in the life of an old man and a dog who walked together down memory lane. We revisited many places I had been, and I told her many stories about my journey. She helped me to dust off many of my life's memories that had long been on the shelf. These pages reflect the new places we visited and things precious to both of us. I would never expect the one who reads this story to be as blessed as I was to live it.

She walked right out of a trash pile and right into my heart. If she was not pretty to anyone else, she was pretty to me. If she was not loved by anyone else, she was loved by me. If she was not worth anything to anyone else, she was worth everything to me. Out of a pile of trash stepped a priceless treasure that walked right into my heart. I loved her so very much.

I thought that I needed to set these things to pen while the path and our footprints on them are still clear. Over time the winds can blow the dust over our tracks, and the windblown snow can hide them in obscurity. One can never imagine how much this trip has meant to me. Rich men would give all of their treasure; poor men would find all their wealth; and hungry men would find their fill on this journey.

> She was like a busy bee that was always buzzing.
> She was like a broken branch that overcame her blemish.
> She was like a faithful fountain that was always flowing.
> She was like a fragranced flower that was always fruitful.

If I were a cake, I would be a plain one, but she came and put the icing on this old man's cake. We invite you to read along. I will try to provide you with a piece of plain cake, and she promises to let you lick the icing from the spoon as she decorates the cake. We hope you are filled.

Chapter 1

LIFE AT THE THICKET

The first time I saw them was at the thicket on the river at a place where rubbish and trash were thrown, things abandoned and discarded, and unwanted intrusions left behind. The erosion of the river literally devoured the roadway. The Louisiana Department of Highways had erected huge concrete barriers to keep travelers from running into this gaping hole, new rights-of-way were acquired for the necessary reconstruction, and the old and new existed side by side.

Away from the gaze of human eyes, the concrete barriers and abandoned section of road sat as a blighted place of hopelessness. A stigma of such proportion was overwhelming and sobering. I first saw them sitting side by side on this abandoned roadway. I could only imagine by the expressions on their faces that when they heard my vehicle approaching they thought the person who had left them was coming back for them.

Their expressions of hope quickly changed to a reaction of fear when I got out of the truck. As I rushed to look beyond the concrete barriers, I watched them disappear into the thicket. The stench of decaying flesh and rotting carcasses of dogs and cats was overwhelming. Discarded household appliances and garbage of all kinds littered this place. I knew that these two fleeing in fear had been abused, neglected, abandoned, and left alone to fend for themselves. Seeing this pathetic pair forced me to consider the course of action that I thought best. Reinforced by the fact that I could end their suffering quickly by killing them, I traveled the mile to my house to get a gun and raced back. Again these two, man's best friends, were sitting side by side waiting in anticipation for the person they would know, the one who had left them. Maybe he had changed his mind and was coming to reclaim them.

They escaped this appointment with death. I never had a chance to pull the trigger. Fear drove them to escape. The thicket once again became their refuge. This cat and mouse game was not over. I waited on the tailgate of the truck to finish what I had come for. I would end their suffering.

Forty-five minutes later a small brown nose barely appeared at the edge of the thicket sixty yards away, then disappeared and reappeared seventy yards away. Fear remained the wedge that separated these two who did not yet trust me. This distance could only continue to grow in this hostile and malignant environment. As this small creature emerged from the thicket, the concrete barrier stood as the only protection from the gun that would claim its life. As it came into full view, I stood and raised the gun. The creature lay on its belly with its head resting on outstretched paws as though it knew the sentence of death was imminent. I walked closer so that I would not miss. What I saw completely disturbed me. Those big brown eyes let me look deeply into this pitiful soul. I realized that I was also looking deep into my own.

At that moment, the similarities we shared began to rapidly emerge. This creature and I had the same Creator: its story is also my story. Life is like a loom. Every experience and circumstance is a thread woven into the fabric of who we are and what we are. As I write these words I am one year short of three score and ten. At the moment I looked into those big brown eyes, I saw a reflection of something that took place in my life forty-five years ago, an experience that now defines who I am and what I am.

On April 14, 1955, the Homochitto River Bridge on U. S. Highway 61, south of Natchez, Mississippi washed away after a tremendous rainstorm leaving a gaping hole. Several people, ignoring efforts to stop them, plunged to their deaths in these swollen waters. How often have warning signs, caution signs, danger signs, and stop signs gone unheeded in our own lives? Nearly ten years later, on a moonlit night, March 21, 1965, the thought of the Homochitto Bridge event led me to consider my own mortality. The One Who created me, Who now rode with me, and Who desired to inhabit me waited for my answer. Not knowing what to say or how to pray, I simply invited Him to continue with me on this journey through life.

The last forty-five years that I remembered in the past forty-five minutes caused me to think about what role I would play in this continuing roadside saga. I was glad that night at the Homochitto River that I could walk away from my past a new man. I came to the thicket as though I was the judge and the jury. Thinking these two pathetic creatures would be better off dead than alive, I found justification in my decision to kill them.

After I saw such a disturbing sight beside the road, it was as though a web was woven, and two probing questions trapped me. Should I forget what I had just seen and go away, and could I live with my decision if I did? It is as if someone unannounced walked into the court of my conscience to plead the case and cause of these two. I went there to end a life, but as I sat there I realized just how sacred life is. Some of life's answers must be found in the heart and not in the head. A rational, logical, analytical, and calculated conclusion may be totally wrong. A man can learn many things about life through the experiences he has had. There is a deeper current flowing in all of life: justice, mercy, and grace. Without these, life would be like a rainbow without color.

A man's conscience is like a shadow that follows him around, like a lingering that will not go away, like the echo of a voice deep within. My search for the answers to some of life's most important questions reminded me of a story recorded in Luke 10:25-37. This story has similarities to my dilemma at the thicket. The Good Samaritan story tells of a lawyer's search for the answers to two questions: "What must I do to inherit eternal life, and who is my neighbor?" Could the lawyer's questions have been prompted by something bothering his conscience?

The man, a lawyer skilled as an orator in tactics of defense and debate, first asked Jesus life's most important question: "What must I do to inherit eternal life?" This question did not solicit a debate from the One who knew the answer; Jesus simply threw the ball back into the lawyer's court when He said, "What is written in the Law, how readest thou?" The lawyer seemed sure he knew the answer to his own question. I can imagine the lawyer standing erect, with arrogance and confidence, saying with assurance: "Thou shall love the Lord thy God with all thy heart, and with all thy soul, and with all thy strength, and with all thy mind, and thy neighbor as thy self."

Jesus told the lawyer he had given a right answer, and if he did these things, eternal life would be his. Sounds easy, doesn't it? Yet the lawyer suddenly seemed to be on the defensive. Out of the blue, as if it fell from the sky, a second question came from the lawyer, "And who is my neighbor?" Many times in life our actions and our answers condemn us. Is some action troubling the lawyer who had appeared so confident earlier? Was the lawyer's love for the Creator and the created deficient? A man can paint himself into a corner at times and be so dogmatic about an answer that he does not leave himself an avenue of escape. Maybe the lawyer needed a heart tune-up. Jesus, the world's Greatest Storyteller, told the lawyer the story of a "certain man" as he passed through the hands of three kinds of people: those who beat him up, those who passed him up, and those who picked him up.

The lawyer listened intently as Jesus told the story of a traveler who left Jerusalem, the City of Peace, to risk his life in Jericho, a place known as a den of thieves in the Storyteller's day. Jesus chose not to name this certain man on purpose because he could be our father, our son, our grandfather, our best friend, our teacher, our business associate, our doctor, or anyone we know. The overwhelming truth is that he could be any of us or he could be all of us. Could he be our neighbor?

The thieves were waiting for this man as they had waited for others who had come before him and as they would wait for others who would come after him. The thieves who robbed the traveler took the clothes off of his back; they took the money out of his pockets; and they beat him until he was nearly dead. The Beater Uppers had done their work. Their mission always the same, the Beater Uppers of the world are waiting on every street and avenue to leave us worse than they found us.

The Good Samaritan story is an earthly story that has a lovely heavenly meaning for us as well as for the lawyer. Jesus' story about the beaten man appeals to a caring heart. Men and dogs, all life is important to the Creator. When the opportunities of life beckon us to make a difference, two probing questions come to mind. If not us, who? If not now, when?

As I sat at the thicket thinking of this story, I decided I could not go away. It was instantly evident to me that these two at the thicket had passed through the hands of someone who beat them up and abandoned them in a horrible condition. I had been drawn to this conflict like a magnet. Which is more important, the life of a man or the life of a dog? It depends on which one we are.

Jesus continued the story of the man who was horribly beaten and bloody, without clothing, near death, and begging for some assistance after his encounter with the Beater Uppers. All the people passing by the badly beaten man ignored him. Even a priest and his assistant passed up the beaten man as they made their way to a beautiful religious edifice that was close by. How could these men in Jesus' story, the called and the chosen, become cold and calloused enough to ignore this case of human suffering?

Do we pass others up in our own lives? Do we join the ranks of the Passer Uppers when we make our flimsy excuses not to become involved? How we respond to those in need is a matter of each individual heart. Often what it will cost us and the hidden dangers that might make us another victim paralyze us, and we end up doing nothing. Since we did not cause the condition, we do not feel obligated and concerned about the solution. Even though these were only dogs, I considered my role in the case by the thicket. They were suffering miserably from the hands of their Beater Uppers. Could I pass them up?

As Jesus neared the end of the story, He described a most unlikely circumstance. A Samaritan appeared, a man who would have been expected to applaud this beaten man's condition. Instead he was appalled by it. Even though Jews and Samaritans had always been bitter enemies, this caring Samaritan could not and would not leave the broken man there. As he listened to the story, the lawyer wondered how this Samaritan came to love his enemy and why he was overcome with compassion. No one would have condemned the Samaritan if he had just passed on by.

My friends all thought I was crazy when they saw what I rescued. These two were the most miserable, hurting, and desolate of creatures. However, something from deep within drew both the Samaritan and me to a place where we could not and would not leave the ones in need on the road.

In an act of benevolence sorely beyond the realm of reason, the Samaritan literally became the way to a new life when he picked up the bruised and broken man, took him to the safety and shelter of an inn, and placed him in the care of the innkeeper. The innkeeper went about each day caring for those who were hungry, hurting, and healing. He set food for the body and soul before the guests, trimmed wicks, and poured oil into the lamps to fuel the flames for the night. The lamp lit the welcome mat, and the sign on the door read, "Whosoever will, may come." The Samaritan and innkeeper both joined the ranks of Picker Uppers.

In this story, Jesus painted a portrait of how each of us can respond to people we meet on the path of life: we can beat them up, we can pass them up, or we can pick them up. There is no way I can explain why I was still beside the road other than to say that it was a Matter of Grace. All of us, the lawyer, the man, the Samaritan, the innkeeper, and the dogs, were searching for answers to some most important questions. The lawyer learned that his neighbor was any person to whom he showed mercy, the "certain man" learned that mercy can come from any unlikely circumstance, and the innkeeper learned that one of life's greatest joys was caring for others.

Some answers can be found in this story; others can be found only in the heart. Love has a way of putting us to the test: do we practice what we preach? A pulse of caring began to overwhelm my heart as I considered these two creatures on the roadside. There would have been no second chance for these two if I had listened to my head. My heart told me that any disrespect for life is disrespect for the Creator. A miracle of mercy is always a Matter of Grace.

The searing words of this story brought such a conviction that a God Thing was about to take place. Memories of my last forty-five years and my forty-five minute wait changed the role I played at the thicket. I went home to get food. When I got back, there was not a sign of this elusive pair that had vanished like ghosts. Their fear of harm was stronger than their pangs of hunger. The shadows of evening visited the thicket, and night came quickly. Knowing the river could quench their thirst, I left food in abundance where it could be found easily.

An early visit to the thicket at the first light showed no sign of life. Could they be gone? The question was still unanswered as I returned home from a day at work. The absence of food in the bowl proved that some creature had been there. The food would keep them from starving for another twenty-four hours. Let this cat and mouse game continue. What would be the outcome of a wager if we bet on who would win this battle of wits between man and beast? Twenty-four hours had elapsed since I first saw them sitting side by side on the abandoned roadway. Would they remember that I provided the food for yesterday? I left no food on this day.

This game became a chess game, a roll of the dice, a playing of all the cards, a challenge that I was about to become a part of a God Thing that began to fuel the fire that is deep within me. On my way to work, I had food and treats in the truck, but I saw no sign of the pair. The bowl sat empty. As I rounded the bend in the road on the way home from work, there they were again, side by side. They did not seem as glad to see me as I was to see them. I wondered where they came from? Who had left them? Why were they left? How would they survive? These were questions best left unanswered because knowing may have caused warring in my soul. The abuse of any creature shows disrespect for the Creator.

As I parked beyond the concrete barriers about sixty yards from where they were sitting, the thicket swallowed them up again.

Wishing to coax them closer, I sat with my back against the concrete barrier with food and treats in hand within arm's reach. I heard the rustling in the vines and grasses, movement so elusive it was hard to detect. The pair must be summoned to a place of surrender. I walked to the place between where they had sat in the open and the place where they had disappeared into the bushes. In these familiar surroundings I placed a bag of unopened dog food hoping that the aroma would draw them out.

There are no adequate words in the human vernacular to describe the condition of these two pitiful, pathetic creatures. They frantically began scratching to open the bag, but they were not in favor of my help and moved away. I retrieved the bag of food and once again sat with my back against the barrier. They took no food from the bowl or out of my hand. The evident pain of hunger had not erased the constant element of fear. The only food they consumed was that thrown on the old abandoned roadway where they could escape in any direction. They consumed each morsel in alternating order. One after the other, they shared the food as though each knew of the other's needs. It was as if they drew strength from each other. A common bond and dependency made them inseparable if only in circumstance.

The expression "a picture is worth more than a thousand words" can well describe what I saw next. The first fleeting glimpses had not prepared me for the feelings and emotions that gripped me. A coldness crept over my heart for the ones responsible for putting them here. A hot anger that screamed for retaliation, retribution, and rebuke engulfed me. Indignation, maybe not of the righteous kind, welcomed me to the place of judge and jury to get even with the perpetrators.

The emaciated male dog was a dog and a half long and a half dog high, a wiener variety pedigreed with no telling what else. Dachshund and others were part of his family tree. The remnants of a black and tan patchy coat were wet from the oozing sores that enflamed his whole body. It looked as if the bones of his hips and ribs would protrude through the skin that was eaten through by the infection in these wounds. There seemed to be no relief from the agony and misery that faced this poor creature.

The very small female dog that had the facial features of a Yorkie and a mixture of some type of wire-haired terrier seemed to be a hopeless case. Abused, neglected, and abandoned, she very likely had found the place that would become her grave, a striking reminder of others left here. Bleeding from incessant scratching, she had open sores all over her body. Her white blood count was elevated because of these infectious sores. Bleeding from the sores had caused anemia. She was skin and bones from lack of nourishment. All these factors contributed to her sad state. She moved with a noticeable limp in her right back leg, and a corneal ulcer threatened the vision in her right eye. Horrible sores caused a constant gnawing, clawing, and scratching frenzy; she needed to find relief from the torment. Sometimes death can be seen as a foe, and in some cases it can be considered a friend.

Except for three hairs on the top of her head, a tuft of hair on the tip of her tail, and hair on the fringes of her ears, she was nearly stark naked and exposed to the elements. How much more could this frail, frantic, forsaken, and fearful creature endure?

Suddenly it was as though another had come to join us, an unexplained presence. Those two just out of my reach felt and heard it too. The petite little female with the big brown eyes and her ears stuck straight out seemed to be searching for sight or sound of this visitor. At the end of the day, these two seemed to be at ease as the darkness came to visit the thicket. I left food and water in the bowls and drove to the house.

"Adios Amigos," I will come again!

Chapter 2

LIFE AT THE HOUSES
OF HEALING

P lans for this mission of mercy found me on the way to the Gowan and Talley Animal Clinic in the town of Winnsboro, Louisiana, early the next morning. George Gowan, DVM, a long time friend, has faithfully cared for our family pets for many years. He has earned trust and respect not just by professionalism but also by personalism. I came to ask his advice, which, from past experience, he knew that I might not take. Though not a veterinarian and certainly unlicensed, I began to diagnose the pair beside the road as having the worst case of mange I had ever seen. Scabs and oozing sores, bleeding wounds with puss and infection, scratching that never seemed to stop, and bodies frail from starvation brought me to this place of healing. "What would or could you do?" I asked. He looked at me like a calf looking at a new gate and as though my mother had dropped me as a baby when she got me out of the cradle. He knew that I had brain surgery in 1989 and that I was brain damaged. Now he must wonder if I was brain dead. "Will you take them as patients?" I asked. There was no response, as if he were deaf.

Before the advent of modern day veterinary medicine, the canine family was treated with some concoction of home remedy. Often mange was attacked with a mixture of burned motor oil and sulfur powder. It is a matter of debate whether the mange mites were smothered to death or killed by some toxic effect of the oil and sulfur. The infestation always seemed to recur, and a cure was nonexistent.

Little did I know that I needed to put the side planks on before loading this wagonload of advice. Dr. Gowan told me there are three kinds of mange: *Démodéctic, Cheyletiella,* and *Sarcoptic* caused by different species of mites. Care should be taken in making a proper diagnosis because other family pets could be at risk of infestation and infection. The safest and most wallet-friendly choice would be to treat the patients at the thicket. I purchased a $37.00 bottle of Ivermectin and received instructions to administer one-tenth cc orally each day for sixty days. This treatment was certainly easier said than done.

The first day of treatment went like this—there was no treatment. I left no food at the close of this day. From this point, the battle of wits only intensified. After I won the Louisiana State Turkey Calling Contest, many hunters sought my advice on how to be successful in killing turkeys. A friend of mine, Billy Joe "Red" West, told me of a ten day struggle where the turkey always outsmarted him. He pointed with the stub of a finger, the victim of a spinning chain when he worked in the oilfields, in the direction of the hang-out of the gobbler and said, "Every time I go down there, I learn something new about that scissor-bill." Then I said to him, "Every time you go, he learns something about you too, and I suspect his learning curve is greater than yours." My learning curve must improve in a hurry or my wager on the battle of wits was in jeopardy.

As I arrived at the thicket after work at the end of day two, the dogs vacated their usual place and both went at the same time to look into the bowl. They were playing me as if I were their fiddle, and I would make their music. They knew the bowl was empty, but they wanted me to know that they needed a handout. My music was their meal ticket. Only, I will not bring it, I thought. You must come get it. I placed two pieces of food into the bowl. Each took a piece, then moved further away. Sitting in the open where they would not be threatened, I offered food from my hand, which they first refused. Driven by the need for food, the small male wiener dog took one piece, then another, and on his third try I nabbed him by the back of the neck. The sickening smell from the sores was a reminder that

25

there must be a cure for this poor soul. I squirted the Ivermectin into his mouth and released him. I had no contact with the little female. The begging of her big brown eyes caused me to throw enough food in her direction to keep her alive until I could come again. The third day was an exact repeat of day two.

Day four found me coming to the fight with more weapons in my arsenal. I brought a dip net of the fisherman variety borrowed from my wife Mary Ann, who uses it to catch baby chicks to cage them for protection against the varmints of night. Armed with food, medicine, and the dip net, I thought maybe the odds of the wager were more in my favor. I had never touched the female, nor had she taken food from my hand. She came close, but not close enough, so she was two days behind the male in taking her medicine. The score was two to nothing.

The next day at work was exhausting, and I did not need another episode at the thicket to erode my patience that was wearing thin. I have concluded that my patience problem must be the result of one of two things: either I played hooky the day it was taught in school, or the school bus driver failed to pick me up for class that day. Patience is something very hard to catch up to if it gets a head start. Patience had a four-day head start, and the outcome of the wager was still in doubt. However, I was encouraged by the fact that I was in the possession of the equalizer, the dip net. I wondered whether they knew what I knew. It ain't over until it's over. The fat lady ain't sung yet. They should just give up. Personally I knew I might give out, but I would not give up.

Sitting with my back once again next to the concrete barrier, I waited for them to get close enough to take food out of my hand. The short-legged wiener mix took one piece and then another. The female mangy mutt was still as elusive as the first day. If patience were a hand grenade, I was in grave danger because I was about to explode. Maybe I needed a patience transplant. The hollow spot in his stomach brought him in reach of the dip net which quickly scooped him up. People could have heard him holler to Memphis, a squalling that would wake the dead, a wailing heard all over Ward 8, Madison Parish, and blood-curdling screams like a panther in the night. These were gosh awful goings on, flopping, yelling, grinding and snapping of teeth, contortions, and madness beyond description. This tirade ended with total exhaustion. He took it like a man, whether willingly or unwillingly, the third dose of Ivermectin. Not to my surprise, there was no one else standing in line waiting her turn. The little female was gone. I left the thicket with the two fugitives still at large. Plan B was becoming clearer all the time. How would I outfox the fox? I left food and drink aplenty. "I will come again," I promised.

It is said with some certainty in the science of mathematics that equations are solved, or unknowns proven, based on some ratio of knowns. From my calculation, the knowns and unknowns of this situation have caused a wreck in solving my problem. I reasoned that one hour at the end of four days equals four hours. Only three doses of Ivermectin per one dog in four days is one twentieth of a sixty-day dose. Twenty times four hours equals eighty hours. If this is what we know, what about what we do not know? Some math solutions are found only in infinity. Was this one of them? Would the goofy female ever take her medicine, and if so, when? The unknowns, the ifs and whens, expedited the implementation of Plan B because death could come to all of us before these two got healed.

I made an appointment with Dr. Gowan to come bleed the mules to run a Coggins test in preparation for an elk hunt in Colorado. How to outfox the fox began. This sage, the good doctor who loaded my wagon with advice before, came to the office to drink my coffee and shoot the bull before going to the farm for the appointment with the mules. I subtly broached the subject with him when I told him I had a patient that he needed to take back to the clinic with him. Because of the lack of an answer when I asked if he would take them as patients the first time, I did not give him the right of refusal this time. Now it is hard for a man to drink my coffee, chew the fat with me, and look me in the eye and say no! Doctors and veterinarians must all take some kind of oath, Hippocratic or hippopotamus or some sort, where they vow to take care of man or beast, don't they?

The night before the appointment I set a live trap behind the barricades at the thicket. A delicious meal of Vienna sausage would surely do the trick. Who would be the first to take the bait? Before I fell asleep, I placed my bet, a wager that I would not have lost. I drove to the abandoned roadway at 4:30 in the morning. With light in hand, I looked as the trap moved toward the river. It was the dumb one, with short legs sticking through the trap, dragging it in an effort to escape to the thicket. Stuck in the vines and bushes, he was now my prisoner and Doc's future patient.

I was not ready for what happened next. When Doc and I rounded the curve on the way to bleed the mules, there they sat again side by side, male and female, pitiful and pathetic, homeless and hurting, and still waiting and watching. Someone unknown who felt sorry for the prisoner had turned him loose, but someone who cared more for him would catch him again. It must be a God Thing for one to be satisfied with being a Picker Upper.

I reset the trap, and he was back in it when we finished with the mules. When the good doctor saw his patient for the first time, the expression on his face said a lot. Being a good mind reader, I knew his thoughts were not about the one captured but rather about me, not only that I was brain damaged but also brain dead.

Fifty odd years ago as a boy, I saw a movie at the Princess Theater, owned by George Elam, in Winnsboro, Louisiana. It was an old black and white flick starring John Wayne. The old cowboy made a statement that left an indelible impression when he said, "There ain't no cure for stupid." Dr. Gowan might have thought "stupid" was my middle name. This is probably a confession that all animal lovers could make, that none of us are quite right. With nothing said, we loaded the patient and live trap, and the hot dog arrived at the Gowan and Talley Animal Clinic in Doc's care a short time later.

Arriving at the clinic later in the day, I was asked by Nan Talley, DVM, the name of the patient in her care. As if I did not hear, I explained that I came to get the live trap to bring the next patient. She stated that the medical records required a name, permission to treat, and the name of the person responsible for payment. Thinking of the long list of newborns announced in the *Franklin Sun,* of Winnsboro, Louisiana, and the *News-Star*, of Monroe, Louisiana, I decided to join the new craze wave of stylish names. The majority of these names will be mispronounced or misspelled on numerous occasions. Careful considerations should be made at births, hospital admissions, roll call at school, baptisms, weddings, and so forth. His proper name I declared to be D'Sidero F'Letatier Al Kareen, and I said that he was registered as such at the courthouse. D'Sidero is his family name, F'Letatier is his French ancestral name, and Al Kareen is his religious name.

Pulling a nine-foot tar-bottomed cotton sack and picking cotton were very valuable educational experiences. The art of expression, something I remembered from the cotton patch, helped in giving meaning to his name. "Now, say his name Man, Man, say his name," and it would go something like this:

D'Sidero – De Side of De Road
F'Letatier – Fount the Tater
Al Kareen – Al Kareem

"The Side of the Road I found the Tater." That's his story and I'm sticking with his name. "What kind of dog it is, man? Man, what kind of dog?" His nickname is The Tater.

Once The Tater was delivered to the doctor, I turned back to the little female. The chilling winds of winter visited the thicket for the first time that fall. Temperatures plunged as the weather front passed with rain predicted in the forecast. I calculated the strategy of trapping this poor little mangy female by thinking how she would think. I set the trap with a liberal serving of roast beef and Vienna sausage; I placed a drape over it to provide a shelter from the wind and rain; and I prayed before leaving that the One who provided for the birds of the air would see her through the night. My concern for her intensified as the sound of the rain on the tin roof grew louder. I thought of how frail, weak, hungry, naked, and sick she was and wondered if this would be the last day of her life. She was so naked that if all of her hair were salvaged it would not make a toupee for a flea, and it was no source of warmth.

I went to get her at midnight, and she was not there. Morning came with no sign of her. No food was missing, and everything was just as I had left it. Someone reported that she was at an armadillo shell just down the road with a half dozen buzzards sitting close by as though expecting her death. With this thought, I went immediately to check the report. There was no sign of life on the road or in the trap. I tended the trap again and added fresh food. This night would be milder because the weather had moderated. I asked the Storyteller to have a happy ending for this story. Mentally and physically exhausted, I was captured by fatigue for the night. At the crack of dawn, I raised the drape covering the cage and there she was. Then this God Thing happened. He let me pick her up. I hope everyone experiences a God Thing someday. Her first master had beaten her, abused her, neglected her, and finally threw her away and abandoned her. This scenario occurs often in the human family, and it too happened to me.

I took her to the house where I live to prepare her for the trip to the veterinary hospital. I used a garden type pump-up sprayer with a mild skin cleansing shampoo, a teaspoon of household bleach, and warm water to spray over her body, taking care not to get it in her eyes. She lay belly down with head lying on outstretched paws, shaking but not scratching, friendly and not fighting, and she seemed to be hopeful and not hateful.

With every fleeting glance, the expression in those big brown eyes was trying to determine if I was friend or foe, stepping stone or stumbling block, and whether I would harm her or help her. As I began to gingerly, tenderly, rinse the dirt and filth from her body with warm clean water, she began to lick herself, either out of thirst or to show me her wounds. I was aware she needed to be moved to a place of healing.

Later Dr. Nan Talley reported on the diagnosis, treatment, and prognosis of The Tater, the dachshund mix, and admitted the new patient for treatment. "What is her name?" I was asked. "Do you want her first name or her back name?" I replied. There would be so much confusion if folks only had one name. I declared her first name to be Mattie and her back name to be Grace. She will always be my Mattie Grace.

We walked to the examination room to evaluate and plan a strategy of action. Skin scrapings confirmed the presence of mange, a corneal ulcer on the right eye, and parasites galore to treat. I saw the handwriting on the wall. There would be a necessary trip to see the banker about mortgaging the farm to pay this bill. I thought maybe Dr. Gowan, who is on the Board of Directors of Franklin State Bank and Trust Co. in Winnsboro, Louisiana, might be willing to co-sign the note.

Many years ago when Herbert Davis was the bank president, I went to see him about borrowing some money. There was a popular advertisement that appealed to the borrowing segment of society. If one needed money to start a business, whether it be a service station, a hamburger joint, a clothing store, or whatever, the slogan said, "See your full service banker." I asked Mr. Davis if they were a full service bank, and he assured me they were. I told him I needed to borrow $600.00, and I would pay it back, $100.00 plus interest per month. He placed the note in the manual typewriter and pecked out the information and terms, passed it to me for signing, and handed me a deposit slip as my record. We talked about other happenings in the community, and then I said I must be going. "Uh," he said, "what was it that you needed the money for?" I told him that I needed it to buy a redbone coon dog and that I was going in the fur catching business. I could have cut his throat, and I do not think he would have bled one drop.

These two companions at the vet clinic suffered from the same sicknesses, and they got the same treatments. The skin scrapings confirmed mange of the *démodéctic* variety. The mite *Demodex canis* caused this condition known as *demodicosis* and was likely passed to them by their mother when they were nursing pups. Of more serious concern was the possible presence of the mange mite *Sarcoptes scabiei canis*. This disease required that a special diligence be maintained due to the highly contagious nature of this mange variety. This disease can infect all ages and breeds of dogs and can be passed to cats, fox, ferrets, and humans. The deplorable condition of The Tater and Mattie Grace suggested that they also had this disease. Because skin scrapings are only positive in about twenty per cent of cases, we erred on the side of caution and isolated them.

We bought large pet carriers which were better homes for them than the thicket. These were their homes in their own room in the big tin-topped house. The Waldorf Astoria could not serve them better. Here they had free room service. If they needed any music,

I played it. The smell of the pine tar shampoo and the Mitaban dip were reminders that this treatment must be repeated until The Tater and Mattie Grace were free from these pests that caused such torment. Dippings and scrapings, dippings and scrapings, dippings and scrapings, until Nan said they were free, free indeed. There was no more scratching; instead, there were an occasional wagging of a tail, healing sores, and new expressions on their faces. If only brown eyes could talk!

Home care and convalescence continued with a steady improvement in their condition. Hair that looked like peach fuzz was as thick as hair on a dog's back. I delivered Tater to his new adoptive parents, Sam and Annette Lewis. He is a retired riverboat captain, and she is a music educator with a beautiful singing voice who would entertain The Tater. Fearful that they would mispronounce or misspell his creative name, I wrote it clearly on a piece of paper: D'Sidero F'Letatier Al Kareem. They changed his name to King of the Hill.

Because Mattie had endured so much misery, I knew she needed a miracle of mercy in her life, and I did not want her memory of Tater to cause her to mourn when he went to his new home. The bond of friendship and kinship is often stronger than any of us can imagine. I assured her that he would have a good home with his new adoptive parents who had changed his name to King. I promised we would see him often.

Building trust is the foundation upon which relationships are built. I would not cheapen the value of trust and assume that Mattie trusted me, but I would spend my energy to earn her trust. The best was yet to come! It was as though she knew and understood that these trips to the vet clinic for dippings and being isolated in the pet carriers were necessary for her healing. I did all I knew to do to soften the effects of the last thirty days for her. I think I celebrated the day of her liberation far more than she did.

Chapter 3

THE GANG WHO LIVES HERE

M attie Grace was no longer under house arrest. She came to the big house with the tall tin roof, and the welcome mat was out when she came. Her ticket to the big house was the reflection I saw the first time I looked into those big brown eyes. She came from a thicket on the river to live in this house.

When Mattie first arrived, I said to her, "This house is so full of life, and I want you to enjoy your stay." I began to tell her there was a menagerie of friends here that came much like she did. "Mattie, they were castaways, throw aways, abandoned, abused, and hungry. They were hungry, not just for food, but also for affection. Mattie Grace, you will never be alone again. We are family." The introductions began and took awhile as I remembered some of the circumstances that brought them here.

We found Buttons at the house where we lived before building the big house. He was a baby kitten lying on his back hissing. He had more than two hundred ticks on him. They were all over him, between all toes, on and in his ears, burrowed in the skin, attached to his lips, and even on another part of his anatomy, his ding-a-ling. My wife picked them off with the tweezers while he clawed like the Tasmanian devil. Lying belly up, he looked like he was wearing a double-breasted suit with two rows of buttons. This is how he came by his name.

There is a common expression "curiosity will kill a cat." Curiosity very nearly killed Buttons. To catch a cat, set a sack or a box with an open top on the floor, or leave a drawer open or a suitcase unzipped, and he will seize the moment. Mary Ann returned from a shopping trip to Wal-Mart, unloaded, and put the groceries in their proper place. She then placed the discarded plastic bags on the patio eventually to ride with Waste Management to the landfill. This curiosity bug that troubles all cats bit Buttons on the back porch. Looking into the Wal-Mart sacks one by one, he thought he had found something. His head got stuck through both handles on one of the sacks. He could not get free, and all havoc broke loose. He thought he saw a booger, a cat-eating monster. Frantic screams and a frenzy, something to be seen on *America's Funniest Home Videos*, began.

There was no sudden end. He overturned and broke pots of flowers as he thought the sound of this noise was about to eat him. As he ran faster from this thing, a collision with the picnic table staggered him. Finally a dash across the yard and back and then a pass through a cedar shrubbery with thick branches next to the corner of the house tore this monkey off his back. This imagined ape had nearly done him in, just one Wal-Mart sack full of surprises. Buttons moved on with us to the big house. "Mattie, this is Buttons. He is one of the old folks who lives here," I said.

Sweetie is an albino, snow white with a pink nose and pads. Clear blue eyes accent her face. I was in Mike's Gun Shop in Winnsboro, Louisiana, when a man charged in and demanded to know who had put a baby kitten in his truck. No one present knew anything or admitted to this happening. A mad man, a belligerent man, is hard to reason with. If he were a whistling teakettle, he would be making a loud noise while letting off steam. This man was doing both.

Trying to defuse this situation, I approached him like the bomb squad and asked, "Did you stop anywhere on your way to the gun shop?" He replied that he had stopped at his sister and brother-in-law's house earlier to drink coffee, then visited a friend's farm shop, and finally stopped at Sullivan's, the local feed store. Sometimes the bomb squad uses a special technique called diplomacy. I said, "It is evident that you don't know much about cats. They are notorious as hitchhikers and have a curiosity that sometimes kills the cat, if you know what I mean." I looked him in the eye and said, "You owe me and everybody in this shop an apology for jumping to conclusions." Jumping to conclusions is the only exercise some people get.

He picked the kitten up by the back legs, raised her up over his head, and said, "I'll knock her brains out on the trailer hitch. Anybody want her?" His behavior reminded me of the south end of a northbound horse.

Then I said, "Give her to me. I'll find her a home, and if you don't go in there and apologize to those men, I'll knock your brains out." Amazingly he made the right choice. As he went reluctantly to apologize to these men, there seemed to be a tint of red on the south end of his horse. I would print his name, but I am afraid that someone would assassinate him. "Mattie, this is Sweetie. She is sweet and lily white."

With a face as flat as a pancake, Jake looks like he had a head-on collision with a wall in a wreck of epic proportions. When he came to us, Mary Ann and I thought he was a refugee from Hurricane Katrina and that someone had lost him in the shuffle of so many moves. The radio announcements, telephone calls to all neighbors, and the lost ads in the newspaper did not produce any admission of ownership. Later one morning a man walked into my office; we poured a cup of coffee; and he said, "Did you find a cat over at your house two weeks ago?" This sounded like a loaded question and suggested he knew more about the situation than I did. I lied when I told him no. He seemed really surprised by my answer. This case of situational ethics continued when I asked him, "Why?"

This ex-preacher started to confess his sins. He met me on the road when I was going home from work. He assumed I had found the cat when I arrived home since he had just left him on the back porch. Mary Ann found the cat frightened and hiding behind a 4x8 foot sheet of plywood on the back porch. Here was another case of a pet being abandoned and thrown away. This cat was now unwanted because he left tracks on the car, shed hair in the house, contributed to allergic reactions, and cost too much to keep.

I asked the man to tell me some things about the cat so that I might recognize him if I saw him. The man began to talk like a parrot. We may learn a lot more from this family parrot if he were sold to the town gossip. He started to spill the beans, and I learned much. He purchased Jake as a weaning kitten for four hundred fifty dollars. He was a tortoise shell Persian with long gold and white hair, declawed so as not to scratch the furniture, and neutered to limit his nighttime prowls. He is now one and one half years old, and his name is Jake. I told the man I would have adopted the cat and given him a good home if he had just asked. He told me how his little daughter C. J. had cried when she had to say goodbye to Jake. I called Mary Ann at her work place and gave her the whole story, but I could never put in print what she called him.

I called the man that night and asked him where C. J. was. She was lying on the couch with her mother watching television. I said to him, "I need to tell you something that she does not need to hear. When I got home from work, I noticed four buzzards in the pecan tree on the south side of the pasture fence. Two others were on the ground as though in a tug-of-war a short distance away. Walking in that direction, I saw the evidence of a great fight. Gold and white hair was scattered everywhere. The two buzzards were pulling on an ear and nose torn from his face." He begged me not to tell C. J., and I told him he was a sorry specimen to mutilate the cat by taking his claws out and throwing him away. I said, "It looked like he had tried to make it to the pecan tree for safety but was unable to climb it after being declawed. He likely fell victim to a mother coyote and her young pack of pups."

"Please," he said, "don't tell C.J." So I hung the phone up and continued my rat killing. Mary Ann had listened to the conversation as I described this horrible ordeal that never really happened. I did not consider this story to be a downright lie, but rather the pulling of his leg. On the order of a Catholic sin, this one was venial and not mortal.

After continuing her dishwashing, Mary Ann came back into the room and asked, "Aren't you going to call him back and tell him you lied to him?" I said, "Nope!" My intent was to expose him for what he was, a Beater Upper. I anticipated that, after hearing my fictitious story, his guilty conscience would keep him from sleeping. At that point, Mary Ann accused me of being as mean as the devil. She was the one who called him names, the kind I cannot put into print. These were the kinds of names for which my mother threatened to wash my mouth out with soap if she ever heard them again. My wife moved from a spirit of condemnation to compassion.

I called again. He answered the telephone in such a rude and crude way, "What do you want?" Thanks to caller I.D., he knew who was calling.

"Where is C.J.?" I asked. "Please do not tell her," he begged. "Please tell her something for me," I said. "There is a gold and white cat lying up here by me on the bed, and he sounds like a well-tuned V-8 engine running, purring like crazy. She can have visitation rights anytime she wishes." I told Mattie Grace, "His name is Pancake Jake."

Booboo came strolling up the driveway one Sunday morning, probably just weaned from his mother, looking like a hobo seeking a handout. As I slipped out the back door, I intended to scare the daylights out of him. He stood at the steps in front of the house looking at the double doors. In a hobo's voice asking for food, he said, "Meow . . . meooow . . . meooooow." He was distracted from looking at the front doors and by the growling in his stomach for food, and I charged his location from behind the house and screamed "boo" as loud as I could. He turned wrong side out. He ran twenty yards before I could say "boo" again to the top of my lungs, and he ran another twenty yards before he heard it. He was nearly running at the speed of sound, 700+ m.p.h. When he realized that the sound was catching up to him, up the tree he went. I laughed so hard I nearly lost my breath. I should have been ashamed to scare him like that. "Booboo, come on down. I won't do it again." He has a beautiful long-haired black coat with not one hair of any other color. He is jet black with gorgeous green eyes. He came here constantly looking for rats, and he is a virtual rat-killing machine. His reputation could earn him a spot in the Rat Killing Hall of Fame. "Mattie, this is Booboo. He is hard to see on a dark night."

Bach has long flowing hair that is a raw steel gray color, and he is a spitting image of Booboo. I have a strong suspicion that they are genetically linked. This kinship is evident by their natural ability to head up the Rat Patrol. I would gamble that both came here in the same vehicle brought by the same person from the same litter, but at different times roughly two months apart. Every time Bach and Booboo apprehend a feed bandit from the barn or other hideout, they bring it to the door as though a celebration of their victory should take place. Each of these gifts is another stinking reminder that they are earning their keep. Bach is not as gifted as Booboo, but he is at least an All-American Ratter, not destined to the Hall of Fame. I said, "Mattie, this is Bach. He is a magician, not a musician."

Tipper rarely goes outside the house. Her comfort is in familiar surroundings. She is colored like a Holstein with bold black and white markings. She demands less attention than any other resident in this place. Her affection is rarely shared and only on her terms. Mary Ann rocks her in the rocker occasionally, combs her hair sparingly, pets her now and then, and feeds her regularly. She seems to be perfectly satisfied even though her demands are few. "Mattie Grace, this is the Holstein, Tipper."

Patches lived in a sharecropper's shack west of Big Creek with a family on Kline Road in Richland Parish, Louisiana. The house burned down in the middle of the night, and this poor family lost all of their belongings and relocated elsewhere. I will never know whether the commotion of the fire trucks with blaring sirens and flashing lights caused her to hide or whether she was left on purpose. North Franklin Water Works, Inc., of Crowville, Louisiana, where I work, has a tank site, water wells, and a booster station a stone's throw from where Patches made her first tracks. I went to check the equipment at this place three consecutive days after the fire. Each time I thought I heard the faint sound of a kitten's cry. Being deaf in one ear and hard of hearing in the other, I could not course the sound or be sure that I had actually heard anything. A day or so later, I saw the movement of something as it disappeared into the ditch off the driveway servicing the tank yard. It was the same sound I thought I had heard before. It was the sound of a kitten, not ashamed for me to hear her cries, yet fearful somewhat of my presence. It is amazing what a can of Cat of Nine Lives will do to eliminate the barriers that exist in circumstances like this.

The next morning she was glad to see me. As I fed her, she climbed up into my lap, and I petted her. Who picked up whom may be debatable for a long time. She is a tabby cat, light orange and gray. She has no desire to explore the outside. I told Mattie, "This is Patches, one who picks no fights."

Muffin is a company cat, having been born literally at the company office in the equipment storage room of North Franklin Water Works. This litter of kittens, eight in number, came as a complete surprise: no sight, no sound, no clue, slam-bam, thank you ma'am. We were the proud owners of the eight kittens, but their mother belonged to the next-door neighbors. The neighbors wanted to assume no responsibility since the kittens were born on our premises. In this ball game, we were the ones penalized without the benefit of the opinion of a referee. Since no lawyer or witness was present, we were given custody with no chance to appeal. Her mother is at it again. This is not her first rodeo, and another litter is on the way. Ride 'em again, catgirl.

Of the eight kittens, none were alike. All were different shades and colors. With the exception of Muffin who was the runt of the litter, we placed them in good homes at no additional charge to water customers who would take them. The expression "little but loud" describes Muffin. A sound like the second floor collapsing onto the first is probably just Muffin knocking over the ironing board. Glass shattering as if a burglar broke out a window means Muffin likely broke all the whatnots in the curio cabinet. She always sounds like a bull in the china closet. Her whereabouts can always be detected by following the loud noises. Pilfering in everything, she breaks the cups and saucers, rattles sacks, and turns over boxes. She is a very small bag of mischief who is always the last to come into the house at night, a requirement for her safety. The perfect gift for Christmas would be an anvil for her, and the bet is that she would break it. I told Mattie Grace, "This is the most destructive cat you will ever see. Muffin is her name."

I found Scooter as a tiny little feller not yet weaned in the middle of Louisiana Highway 15 in front of Representative Noble Ellington's office. Two scenarios seemed likely. Either he fell out from under someone's car, or his mother could have dropped him transporting him from one location to another. A broken leg and hip injury temporarily paralyzed him. He was unable to move, and his chances of survival in the middle of this busy four-lane highway were as likely as a snowball in a hot place. I put my flashers on, yanked the door wide open, blocked the traffic, put him in a small box on the front seat of the truck, and took him to Mary Ann for advice. The psychologist in me had a flash of brilliance when I used this end around play called reverse psychology. "Reckon I ought to just knock him in the head," I said. Her eyes crossed just before I heard the answer. Without going into the details of the answer, she left with tires squealing on the way to Rundell Veterinary Hospital in Monroe, Louisiana. Jim Rundell, DVM, put a steel pin in the right back leg and fashioned a splint from a flimsy wire coat hanger. The kitten's name came from the fact that he looked like he was riding on a scooter. This injury caused him to walk with a stiff right back leg as though he were peg-legged with his tail cocked over to the right like a rudder to balance him. His color is hard to describe. It is an iridescent gray with vertical stripes. These stripes appear, then disappear, and reappear as he moves in the sunlight. He is my partner in crime.

Our debilitating addiction to Blue Bell ice cream has left us both overweight. Knowing that our health was in jeopardy, Mary Ann once put us both on a diet saying it was for our own good. There is nothing good about having to give up Blue Bell ice cream. Other addictions are probably easier to overcome. Malnutrition began to take its toll on me. First, two pounds, then five, then ten, and then the rigors of withdrawal reduced my weight by fifteen pounds. These last three months on our diet, Scooter has not lost one ounce. I wondered why, and I found out.

When we moved to the big house, we moved an old chest type freezer that was worn out when we got here. It finally gave up the ghost, and we purchased a new one. It fell my lot to discard the old one and put all the contents of the old into the new. I discarded meats, vegetables, fruits, and nuts dated over three years. While checking all the freezer contents, I found two black heavy-duty garbage bags filled with a passel of answers about our weight loss. The elimination of Blue Bell was not our diet, Scooter's and mine. Instead, it was my diet. The reason Scooter was still gaining weight was not a thyroid problem. He still came every night at 9:15, or an hour on either side when the time changed. He sounded like the horn on a tugboat, "Honk . . . hoonk . . . hooonk." His salivary glands became active like Pavlov's dog. When I looked into those black bags from the freezer, it did not take a rocket scientist to figure out that I had been had. Mary Ann hid the ice cream from me, but not from Scooter. Scooter's other passion is drinking water by jumping into the bathtub with a small dripping stream where he licks and laps it until his belly is full. I continued with the introductions, "Mattie Grace, you will love Scooter, and he will love you. Always remember we are family."

"Mattie, nine cats in one house can stack the deck against one little lightweight dog. You better get to pumping iron and get a Charles Atlas or an Arnold Schwarzenegger physique, or you will need to get your bluff in on them right off the bat. You have to win the first fight, or it will be a long row to hoe for you." It was not long until Mattie ruled the roost and the cats roosted in the windows, on counters and shelves, on top of furniture, and in cracks of the closets. The exception was Scooter who had no fear of man or beast, a lover and not a fighter, who loved everybody. The diverse nature of this gang was a source of much humor and entertainment. As Mattie began to mix and mingle with this bunch, I began to marvel at the miracle of her life. I was the one who extended a hand to give her hope for healing that restored her health and brought her to a home where she could find happiness. Mattie's presence was like turning on a light bulb. Energy and enthusiasm filled the house.

Chapter 4

MANGE, LEPROSY, AND SIN

Mange

Mattie Grace came to the big house blighted by a horrible canine disease called mange, a condition that probably caused her first owner and master to abandon her by throwing her away. Her deplorable state, not of her choosing or any fault of her own, was likely inherited by association from her mother as a nursing pup. As her sickness grew worse and worse with each passing day, her master must have come to the conclusion that her cure was not worth the cost. She was thought to be no more than a bag of trash to be thrown away and discarded. One man's trash is another man's treasure. When I stood to raise the gun to end her misery and suffering, I saw the reflection in those big brown eyes whose worth could never be measured in dollars and cents. The sight was both breathless and priceless as I now looked on what was and what was to come. Beauty is in the eye of the beholder. I did not look on what she was, but rather on what she would become. Matthew 13: 45-46 says, "Like the merchant who was seeking goodly pearls, who when he had found one pearl of great price, went and sold all that he had, and bought it."

Mattie was just a hand-me down, hand-me around dog. The experience of the last few weeks was so traumatic for her. A total stranger caught her, passed her on to the shampoos and dipping vats at the veterinarian's office, and placed her under house arrest to protect her and the other pets. Her life was changing at such a rapid pace that she was not able to fathom it all. The look of bewilderment, confusion, emptiness, and uncertainty filled her eyes with sadness.

So many people in our society are hurting just like Mattie Grace was hurting when I first saw her. Think of the many children who, through no fault of their own, have been abandoned, abused, and neglected by their own parents. Divorce, alcohol and drug abuse, a tragic death, loss of a livelihood, a catastrophic health consequence, and family feuds that fester tear families apart and can lead people into a life of depression, danger, destruction, dishonor, division, despair, and disrepair.

When life seems to fall apart, the way out is always heart first, not head first. When things of life seem to box us in and corner us up, the fixit in us wants us to figure it out. We simply ring up the head and ask what it is going to do about this. The reason that many circumstances and problems are not solved is that when our head tells us to consult our heart, we downright refuse. Hardheaded and bull-headed are the terms for a head that is out of tune with the heart. How much better would life be if we listened to our hearts? The healing for all of us is when our heads and our hearts are in harmony.

As I went down to the utility room to get Mattie Grace out of the pet carrier that had confined her for the last twenty-eight days, I felt so guilty I had put her there. Several times a day Mary Ann and I would visit her to tell her that things were getting better. A valuable lesson we all need to learn is that we cannot protect the ones we love from the pain that will heal them. I picked up two towels and a washcloth and opened the door to her cage with the promise that she would not have to stay here again. She looked like a little ragamuffin, somewhat like a Raggedy Ann doll, when I picked her up this time. The sores and scabs were gone. She had scars left from open wounds and a limp that never seemed to hinder her. I figured she would carry these to her grave. Mattie Grace was a miracle.

I held Mattie and sat down on a small milking stool that had belonged to my Granny Collier. Her clay crock churn with its plunger was close by in the corner. These objects brought back wonderful memories of Granny when she let me sit in her lap and make butter with this very churn. The Big Book she held on her lap, more times than she held me, was a source of many stories I heard at her house.

Leprosy

"Mattie, Grandma Collier told me a story about Naaman who was captain of the servants of the king of Syria. Naaman was a leper. His sickness was very similar to your disease." Sickness can come to the good and the bad, the rich and the poor, the deserving and the undeserving, and it is no respecter of persons. Life dealt Naaman a hand that he wished he did not have to play. Since life is not a game of poker, he could not fold the cards he was dealt. This man, who was a picture of success still on top of his game with unlimited resources at his disposal, was now at once broke and broken. How quickly can the worm turn? He had become a leper.

The answer to his own healing was in the house where he lived. After the Syrians had made a conquest of Israel, a young woman was brought captive to be an attendant to Naaman's wife. In a conversation with Naaman's wife, the young maid revealed the possibility of a cure. It was amazing that she was not bitter over her circumstance and that her heart wished healing instead of harm. She must have listened to her heart instead of her head.

She told her mistress, Naaman's wife, of the reputation of a prophet in Samaria that could heal Naaman of his leprosy. When this news reached the King of Syria, he drafted a letter to the King of Israel asking the King to cure Naaman of his leprosy. The King of Syria sent along gold, silver, and clothes as payment for this favor. The King of Israel misunderstood this request. He evidently knew nothing of the prophet the little maid had talked about. This request frightened the King of Israel because he thought it might be a trap. He also wondered if he failed whether the Syrians would return, ransack their land, and impose a sentence of death on him. He may not have known how to pray or what to say, but try he did. "Am I God, to kill and to make alive," he said, realizing that this task and assignment were bigger than he was. The prophet Elisha bails out his boat to keep it from sinking, saying, "Send him to me that he shall know that there is a prophet in Israel."

With the horses pulling his chariot, Naaman came to the front door of Elisha's house. The prophet sent his messenger to Naaman with these instructions: "Go and wash in the Jordan seven times, and thy flesh shall come again to thee, and thou shalt be clean." A temper tantrum of epic proportions ensued, a madness that was fueled by the fact that the prophet did not personally come, but instead sent a peon. Naaman went away in a rage threatening to dip in the rivers of Damascus. My father always said a man who doctored on himself had a fool for a patient. Those who loved and served Naaman offered him some advice in the form of a question, "If the prophet had bid thee do some great thing, wouldest thou not have done it, how much rather then, when he saith to thee, wash, and be clean?" Naaman almost listened to his head and would have been a fool, but others who loved him were helpful in getting him to listen to his heart. His heart brought about his healing as he dipped seven times in the Jordan River, and he was clean. Fortunately for Naaman, he listened to others. (II Kings 5:1-27)

"Mattie, it was good news when Dr. Gowan said you could be healed because it was once thought that your disease was incurable. Mattie, the dippings were not that bad. You are clean. You heard the One I heard at the thicket that day, a presence neither of us could see. Your ears stuck straight out, and you looked with those big brown eyes as though He would appear out of the air. During the night that it was so cold and the rain fell on the tin roof, I asked Him, the Storyteller, to have a happy ending to your story. He let me pick you up the very next morning. You were then a hand-me down, hand-me around dog. The people I handed you to, Doctors Gowan and Talley, are my friends and an extension of my caring. Gold, silver, and clothing were offered to the prophet Elisha for Naaman's healing. Some people would give everything they had just to be well. Namaan's healing cost him nothing as the prophet refused any payment. What these two, Dr. Nan and Dr. George, did for you can never be measured by dollars and cents. They made you clean."

Leprosy is an infectious disease that has been known since biblical times. It has affected humanity for over 4,000 years and was recognized in ancient civilizations of Egypt, India, China, Somalia, Japan, and others. Leprosy, also known as Hansen's disease, is named for the work of Gerhard Armauer Hansen, a physician. Leprosy is caused by the organism *Mycobacterium leprae* with two common forms, *tuberculoid* and *lepromatous*. The *lepromatous* form, the most feared form, is thought to be incurable. Early detection of the disease and its treatment have made great strides since the 1930s. Drugs like Dapone, Rifampicin, Minocycline, and Ofloxacin have all been helpful in arresting this disease. There has been some concern about a drug-resistant strain of *Mycobacterium leprae*; therefore, a global watch is underway.

The human condition called leprosy causes so much misery and suffering by those afflicted and affected. The sentence of society has long been one of rejection, banishment by family and friends, ostracism, and a wandering lonely existence. Even though it may not be a sentence of death, the one defiled was always considered unclean, and the scars are indelible marks branded in his flesh forever. In earlier times, the priest, not a physician, determined the fate of a suspected victim. Often a very thin line existed between the clean and the unclean, between the maybes and the maybe nots. A judgment pronounced could often very likely be wrong. I have thought of the many times that I thought I was so right, only to later discover I was so wrong. The priest alone would declare the person unclean. Just like the snap of the fingers, a person's life was forever changed; the wind was taken out of his sails. The judgment was like a sucker punch to the gut.

Often we have been quick to rush to judgment and realize we were wrong when we learned the rest of the story. Before voting, please consider the outcome. The leper must reside outside the camp, apart from family and friends, and sometimes in the presence of other pitiful souls who served as constant reminders of his own condition. This community of cripples had all of human dignity squeezed from their lives. Anyone who ventured near was admonished to stay away. The leper would place a covering over his lips and cry in a loud voice, "Unclean, unclean, do not come near, I am unclean."

The afflicted and affected, the leper, his family, and his friends, were separated from each other through a life-altering verdict. As he thought of loved ones, they thought of him; he could not minister to them and they could not minister to him. Lonesome was a two-way street. The needs of each must be met by another. A leper would neither hold his wife in his arms again nor embrace or shake hands with a friend. He forever lost the joy of giving a daughter away in marriage, and he would never rock a grandchild to sleep or tussle with a son in fun.

Life can change so abruptly. It can consume and devastate us. There are some circumstances in each of our lives where I cannot help another, and he cannot help me. Often in life, when I have been at the end of my rope, the resources in my possession were not sufficient for the situation. I have not been left alone on my journey. The One I invited to come along with me on my journey has never failed to be present when I needed Him. I can say, "Thank you for being there when I needed You most."

Mange, leprosy, and sin are birds of a feather, kinfolks of sorts, because of the impact and life-altering consequences of each. Not only do these affect the afflicted but also every one who comes in contact with them.

Mattie's mange cost her her health. It very nearly cost me my wealth, but this pearl of great price was a great bargain. The leper's leprosy robbed him of the things we all sometimes take for granted.

Sin

Preachers spend much time talking about sin. According to some accounts, some preachers know a lot about sin, and some know little. It is a heap better not to know much about sin than to have much experience with it. Whoever said "sin will take you farther than you intend to go, and sin will keep you longer than you intend to stay, and sin will cost you more than you intend to pay" did not lie. Once sin gets its grip on a person, it does not want to turn him loose. The devil has trolled the bait by many folks who in a moment of weakness took it. When sin happens, people respond in one of two ways. Most will try to cover it up while only a few will confess it. Confession is God's way to cure sin.

Sin affects everybody, not just some. Do we want to talk about someone else's sin? It is a lot less painful to talk about our mother-in-law's sin, or our wife's or husband's faults, or our neighbor's mistakes, or the preacher man's indiscretions than to talk about our own sin. Because sin will tell on us, we had better be careful. We may open a Pandora's box or a new can of worms, enter a house of horrors, or recognize someone familiar in the mirror. We must be careful that the skeletons in the closet are not ours. Because sin will tell on us, we must know our sins will find us out. No matter how hard we try to outrun sin, it will be there when we arrive. We can never win a fistfight with sin. It will beat us up and skin us up. Sin hurts. It will always make us say "OUCH!"

Having attended services in many different denominations, I have noticed a commonality toward the end of every service. A time referred to as an invitation, confession, decision time, altar call, or some other Holy happening occurs. The God representative's appeal is never to come and confess the sins of another. Sin always has a payday. It is like the Fram oil filter commercial, "Pay me now or pay me later."

Sin never struts around in international orange. It wears camouflage clothing. The sin problem can never be cured by the head. Its healing comes from the heart. If we listen to the head about sin, it will tell us to cover it up. Listen to the heart, and it will tell us to confess it.

Sin is the hell-deserving leprosy of the soul, a universal curse that has only one cure. That one cure is the serpent in the wilderness, the lamb of the Passover, the shepherd of the sheep, the water in the well, the bread of heaven, the lamb of God, the door, the light of the world, the resurrection and the life, the alpha and omega, the author and finisher of our faith, the way, the truth and the life, and his name is Jesus. The cure for this curse is found in Acts 4:12: "Neither is there salvation in any other, for there is none other name under Heaven given among men, whereby we must be saved."

Mange, leprosy, and sin eat like a cancer at one's dignity, health, and wealth until there is nothing but a shell left. The coming of death is a miserable visitor. Sin will see that death will knock on our door one day.

I told Mattie another of Granny's stories about Jesus and the Disciples. They had just finished the Passover meal as they remembered how the innocent was slain as a sacrifice for the guilty. He took a towel, laid aside His garment, and wrapped it around Himself. He then poured water into a basin, intending to wash the feet of all who were in the room. As was his custom, Peter put his mouth in gear before his brain. Like Peter, we often get into trouble when we speak before we think. Peter said, "Thou shalt never wash my feet," and again, "Though I should die with thee, yet will I not deny thee." Both times he had to eat his words, a bitter pill to swallow. Jesus said, "If I don't wash thee, thou hast no part with Me." Peter then said, "My feet, my hands, my head," expressing a willingness to be washed all over. "Mattie, think before you speak because your ticket to the big house is your willingness to be washed all over."

I held Mattie and cradled her in my arms to carry her up the stairs. A faint smell, the residual of the chemical used to treat her, was evident. We climbed the stairs in the great room. Whether or not she had an intense interest in the story or the surroundings, Mattie was glued to the moment. After reaching the landing at the top of the stairs, we could choose to walk through either of two doors to enter the living suite. I stood here when this house was only a dream and visualized what it is today. The dream, the design, the engineering, the architecture, the building, and the resources emptied me out of blood, sweat, and tears. This territory is familiar to me—the kitchen, the pantry, the bathroom, the bedroom, the closets, and the sitting room.

As I knelt down on my knees, I put Mattie on the floor once again in an unfamiliar place. Though the welcome mat was missing, she sensed its presence. "Mattie," I said, "Welcome home, take a look, and see what you think." I took a seat in a chair to read the daily newspaper and let her explore without interference from me. She went from room to room and back again. She would glance in my direction in passing, though not looking me directly in the eye when she passed. She did this several times, and I noticed a sort of transformation. Her ears went from hanging limp to flying at half-mast, and her eyes from a flicker to a full flame. Having heard the expression "a penny for your thoughts" I would have given much more for hers. She came and sat directly in front of my chair, this time to look me squarely in the eyes. I knew she wanted me to pick her up.

Not knowing what to expect, I put Mattie into the bathtub. Would she object like Naaman, the leper, or submit to this rite of cleansing for her health and healing like Peter? As though she were commanded, she took the bath like a little soldier. Animals of the pet variety all seem opposed to the persuasion of bathing, often with violent objection. It was as if she not only heard but also heeded the stories I told her. The warm water rose in the tub slowly climbing up her legs until it reached her belly. She seemed to welcome the washcloth used to squeeze the water on her sides, back, head and face. I gently rubbed shampoo, one medicated and another fresh fragranced, into thick rich lather and tenderly applied it to her skin still sensitive from her ordeal. As the suds and dirt disappeared into the drain, she began to lick the clean water from her skin and from my hands, maybe from thirst or as a gesture of approval. The curse of mange cured, she was clean.

The two towels brought from the utility room dried us both. As I dried her with Mary Ann's hair dryer, she was as quiet as a mouse. She smelled like a bouquet of freshly picked flowers. I picked her up and put her on a pillow on our bed. She curled up into a little round ball. The texture and length of her hair reminded me of a longhaired coconut. She would not win Best of Breed, let alone Best of Show, at any dog show. Her worth was not in what I could see, but in what I could not see. Her mail would now go to a new address because she came from a thicket on the river to live in this house.

Mattie seemed to be perfectly content as she lay curled on the pillow on this graduation day from the pet carrier that had housed her and transported her to the animal clinic. Twenty-eight days of treatment had brought a horrible chapter in her life to an end. Suffering from agony beyond description, scratching at the source of suffering, and a stomach never satisfied from hunger, she was thrown away like a soiled diaper. Would she look back on her life at the thicket and think perhaps she had won the lottery? She is the story of one who had come from rags to riches. I turned the light out, patted her gently, and said, "Good night, Mattie Grace."

This night reminded me of the first night we brought our son home from the hospital after his birth forty-one years ago. When they sleep, a baby and a puppy mimic the same sounds: squeaks, gurgling sighs, small grunts, gaspings, rattling, and arrested breathing that will scare us nearly to death. Mattie was no different with her breathing. Then, after a gentle touch, she would continue with another breath. Buttons, Jake, and Sweetie were fast sleep in their baskets in the bathroom. No sounds came from them.

Chapter 5

THE ALARM CLOCK

A tranquil night suddenly took an about face and a complete turn around. This little lamb that had been asleep on the pillow now acted like a raging lion. Barking, growling, snapping teeth, and in a frenzy, she scared me out of ten years of growth. I turned on all the lights in the room to see what had happened. The cats had gone to higher ground in the recesses of the closet. The expression on Mattie's face suggested that she had experienced a nightmare. Maybe it was a memory of a near death experience from when she lived at the thicket or a flashback of some kind.

Looking and listening in the direction of the great room, she stood in the middle of the bed, not at ease, but rather at attention like a soldier or sentry on guard. We both heard it simultaneously. This sound was familiar to me, but this was probably the first time she had been exposed to it. "Mattie, sweet Mattie," I said, "it is just the alarm clock. It slipped my mind to tell you when I introduced you to the other family members."

To calm and soothe her, I picked her up in my arms and carried her still shaking down the stairs. The alarm clock was still doing his thing with at least every other breath. "Mattie, don't be afraid, this is Little Man, and he is just doing his job. His companion is Little Hen. He has earned his keep at this house and is part of the family." I had forgotten to introduce them with the gang who lived here.

Little Man is a tiny B. B. Red Bantam born here on the farm. Others came before him and others after him, but none have ever come like him. Little Man has been voted chicken of the decade. He is truly a super chicken, small in body, but big in heart. One of the barnyard bullies spurred him in his right eye, and he is too fragile to defend himself. He is a true and faithful Picker Upper. I saw him take nine baby chicks whose mother abandoned them and cover them with his wings on the roost so that they would not freeze to death. He repeated this act of kindness with four babies another time, and finally he did the same for Little Hen. Mary Ann and I decided that only death would separate Little Man and Little Hen. They are placed each day in a secure 10x10 pen in the back yard and returned to the house at the close of the day.

George Gowan, DVM, and Nan Talley, DVM, partnered up in the veterinary business several years ago. There has always been a feeling among the old timers that a rite of passage had to be earned by the new kid on the block. That would be Dr. Nan at that moment. Little Man has the longest spurs I have ever seen on any nationality of chickens. In a country boy's vernacular, they are humongous. On putting him out this day and noticing that he had shed one of his spurs, I decided to take him with me. Occasionally I let him ride with me because he would crow on demand. All I had to say was "Talk to me, Little Man," and a crow would be forthcoming.

The trip took us to the courthouse, the Clerk's office, the Assessor's office, the Sheriff's office, and the barbershop; Little Man really put on a show. As I passed by the veterinary office, I saw all the girls standing outside. I could not tell if they were smoking, dipping snuff, gossiping, or enjoying the sunshine. Since I had not met Dr. Talley, I thought that this time was as good as any for her to earn her rite of passage. This rite of passage is a first cousin to the ritual of hazing by fraternities and sororities. She might remember this from her college days.

I concocted the following story when I asked, "Is the doctor here?" Dr. Nan Talley threw her hat into the ring when she said, "What can I help you with?" I went on to say, "The Deep South Rodeo is in town, and I am between a rock and a hard place. I am supposed to perform with my trick rooster during the bull-riding contest. He spins on a stick with his spurs and crows while doing it." I handed her the shed spur, pointed to the bloody stub, and asked her if she could help.

She had never had a chicken for a patient and hinted that this may be beyond her expertise. With tears in my eyes, I made it plain that the free tickets they offered me would go down the drain if something were not done. I suggested Super Glue or Derma Bond only to hear the rocks rattle in her head when she shook it to say No! The story goes that she called Dr. Gowan who was vacationing in Taos, New Mexico. Nan reported that a crazy man was seeking treatment for a chicken, a very strange request.

"Nan, what did he look like?" the good doctor said. As he listened for her reply, there was a long pause before he commented, "Dr. Talley, you have just been had. You have just met Marion Collier!" He had only to guess but one time to name the culprit.

The reputation of Little Man has spread far and near. Some of my friends, the gossiping kind, have told of his position of importance as the alarm clock for our household. Others always approach this report with skepticism, ridicule, cynicism, disbelief, and consider it a downright lie. On traveling to various locations, I noticed a peculiar thing began to take place. People would not ask about Mary Ann, her health, or her well being. Instead the comment would be like this, "How's the rooster?" Thinking this question to be strange and queer, I would ask, "Why?" Friends who visited and stayed with us spread the word that indeed I had a live alarm clock in my house.

A colorful rooster, little but loud, announces the coming of day, every day in this house. "Mattie, if you want to give someone a nice house-warming gift that they may not have, consider a live alarm clock."

A lot of houses are filled with parrots, parakeets, and canaries. These are no more than mere ornaments and trinkets that only decorate a place. These birds just make a mess and serve no useful purpose. Little Man is the real deal. He is bright and beautiful. He works any time and all the time. Other people have clocks they have to wind up, set to proper time and alarm, and buy electricity or other power sources. The batteries that run most clocks are Ray-O-Vac or

Delco Energizer, but my alarm is Eveready because he is ready all the time.

"Mattie," I said, "country folks or city slickers, take your pick, but there are a few advantages of a country boy's alarm. If someone comes to my house and stays longer than he is welcome, I just slip out to the great room, turn on the light, and the party is over. Or I can shine the flashlight on the pen and the racket begins. This trick can be done any time of night, on the hour, the half hour, or in between. Mattie, a lot of life's lessons are learned in the simple things. Sophistication can cause one to thumb his nose up in arrogance and cause a feeling of holier than thou. Mattie Grace, this is Little Man and Little Hen. I'm so sorry I forgot to introduce them along with the cats."

Chapter 6

THE REST OF THE GANG

M attie began the next day with the rousing announcement by Little Man, who kicks the ball everyday to start the game. The alarm was like the whistle of the referee who puts the ball on the tee and says, "Let the game begin." About an hour and a half after we were abruptly awakened by the live alarm clock, Little Man and Little Hen were in the yard pen enjoying the warm sun of this beautiful day. We could say the day was in full bloom and that a tour of the farm might be eye opening, interest arousing, and therapeutic for Mattie. Not knowing how she would respond, I used a collar and leash to guarantee her safety and security.

Some of the most enjoyable experiences of my early years were the times when our family visited a wildlife park, an animal museum, a farm, or a zoo. It was here that we made our first contact with the wild animal world, some native, some foreign and exotic, and the domesticated animal kingdom that lives in harmony with man. The encroachment of the human race and catastrophic environmental changes have contributed to the reduction and sometimes extinction of many species. If it were not for the dedicated work of the curators, directors, and keepers of these facilities, many people would never experience this great journey of learning. There ought to be a shared responsibility because all of us are "Keepers of the Zoo." I wondered how Mattie would respond to this tour.

Not willing to let her explore on her own as when we put her down in the second floor living suite, I carried her to the back porch in my arms, and I talked to her as I would my child. "There is so much more. Let's go see the rest of the gang." Standing on the porch, I showed her a sight rarely seen, proof that those who live here are family. A big black dog was lying in the warm rays of the sun holding a big iridescent cat in his arms.

Meg was a stray pup found on the Elam Woods Road nearly twelve years ago. No thicker than the width of my hand at first, she is now grossly overweight. She is black with a small white patch on her throat, and her heart protects her family. I told Mattie that Meg and Scooter were always close to each other. "You would never expect a dog and cat to be best of buddies like these two. Don't be afraid. They'll join us on the tour, and you'll enjoy their company." I knelt with her next to Meg and Scooter and put her on the ground watching as the chemistry of friendship developed. Often in chemistry, one more addition to the formula can have disastrous reactions. These three soon were known as the Three Musketeers of the Farm: "all for one, and one for all."

Fowl words filled the air. From every direction came fowl, fowl words. Voices of excitement and objection caused Mattie to look around and see whether I was still on the end of the string. We hear these loud obnoxious noises anytime a stranger is on the premises, a varmint comes around, a hawk is heard or seen, or a serpent spied.

"Mattie, they are better than watch dogs, these things called guineas." Guineas are probably descendants of the guinea fowl from the continent of Africa brought by early settlers to this country. They are hyper and nervous creatures running here and there chasing bugs, looking for snakes, and working as exterminators of spiders, frogs, worms, and other pests around the farm. "Mattie," I explained, "it was a custom years ago when I was a boy to dye colorful Easter eggs and enter them in a contest at school to be judged for best decorated." Usually we made a challenge to see whose egg was the hardest. Contestants lined up and bashed two eggs together. The broken egg became the property of the winner. This contest was repeated until the winner had all the broken eggs and the bragging rights to the hardest headed egg. "Mattie, team up with a country

57

boy and rob a guinea nest. A city slicker could never beat you in this game with a store bought egg."

Then we saw chickens galore, too many to number. Their numbers are constantly changing with new hatchings and varmint casualties so that a tally is always inaccurate. The census of chickens exceeds more than two hundred. The fascination of this situation is found in the philosophy of the madam of the farm, Mrs. Mary Ann. Maybe her belief in monogamy has caused the chicken ratio of fifty/fifty, one rooster to one hen. Anyway, it makes no sense to me. She sees no humor when I tell her that King Solomon had a harem of seven hundred wives and three hundred concubines and that I thought it okay if I did also. When I said that, Mary Ann asked if I had read what happened to Solomon. I said, "Yes, he slept with his fathers."

"No," she said, "How did he die?" The theologian in her read between the lines and told me that one of his wives shot him and the same thing would happen to me if I thought I could get away with this kind of behavior.

"You see what I mean, Mattie, about her having no sense of humor. I was just using this story to help her see the light and understand that we had entirely too many roosters." This little woman with a short fuse acts as though she has a bullet with my name on it, and she might enjoy using it. "Mattie, my friend Roy McDuffie says if she shoots me, no charges would be filed. Only a day of celebration, a crown, a scarlet robe, and a scepter would be her reward for what she has to put up with. Mattie, that's just his opinion."

Chickens galore mean eggs galore collected by the five gallon buckets full. We give these eggs to neighbors, friends, and strangers. Having lost count of how many starts of chickens we have placed in foster homes, we know that the count is considerable. Since many women do not like to take advice from their husbands or have a Come to Jesus meeting, I have thought we need to enlist the help of some consultants to advise us on the continually growing chicken situation on the farm. An economist, a marketing expert, an accountant, and a financier may help me with this ongoing debate with this irate woman. Sorry, I forgot the marriage counselor.

I made it clear to Mary Ann that if she could interpret passages from the Bible, so could I, and that in the thinking department, she was weaker than I. My argument was that roosters do not lay eggs; roosters eat feed. None of our chickens are ever fried or made into dumplings. Caring for chickens takes a lot of time and a lot of money to buy scratch grain and medicine. After this clashing of the minds, all decisions regarding our large chicken population were vetoed by the Madam of the Farm. I said, "Mattie, I'll say this to anyone. If you need a special gift, you should consider a live alarm clock. We'll furnish the rooster, but he must be kept in the house at night. Mattie, this place is wall to wall chickens."

Next I introduced Mattie to Willie, a 1993 model molly mule I purchased from Charlie Cecil Brown of Crowville as Mary Ann's twenty-fifth wedding anniversary present. Mr. Brown, a long time friend, had a fine stable of Missouri fox trotting horses that he showed and rode proudly. He envisioned raising some gaited mule colts. The first two were born on the farm during William Jefferson Clinton's watch. Cecil promptly named them after the President of the United States of America. One he called Slick, and the other he called Willie. Thus they became known as the Slick Willie Team.

With a bit of persuasion from me and with the knowledge Willie would have a good home, Mr. Cecil Brown delivered her on the day of her weaning as a four-month-old colt. She quickly adopted us and quit crying for her mother. She is what the old timers referred to as a Jesus Cross Mule because of a dorsal stripe down her back and a cross just behind her forelegs down her sides. Tiger stripes decorate all four legs.

"Mattie, mules are strange creatures. They are the only animals that can be extinct one year and have a million or more the next year because they are hybrids. A jack donkey and a mare horse produce mules; a horse stallion and a jenny donkey produce a hinny mule."

A known mule breeder from north Mississippi shed some valuable light on the development of mules as working animals in the United States. Wild African asses captured on the plains of the Serengeti were bred to mares from this continent to produce the first mules. Some years later, the king of Spain sent a Catalonian or Spanish Jack, named Royal Gift, to George Washington to breed on his plantation at Mount Vernon signaling the birth of the modern American mule. The wild African asses had crosses on their backs. This cross is the signature that Willie carries from her African ancestors. This basically mild natured docile animal that can blow up at the drop of a hat has always been a mystery to me. These blow-ups are only beneficial to the orthopedic surgeons who charge exorbitant fees to fix the victims of these wrecks. "Mattie, Dr. Gowan thinks either me or Willie has a loose screw, but due to patient and doctor confidentiality, he can't say which one."

The animal psychologist in me thinks there must be an explanation for the glitch in Willie's behavior. The answer lies in my theory of reincarnation. In a previous life, a wild African lion ate Willie. Now if she looks at a stump, or a log shaped just right, or a bush full of breeze, or a porcupine, or an English bulldog, or whatever else she pulls out of her hat, she may just have a blow up thinking that she has seen another lion.

The first wreck happened several years ago at the Deep South Rodeo in Winnsboro, Louisiana. I had taken Willie there on request of the bull-fighting rodeo clown who wanted to ride her in the grand entry. After saddling her, I was going to warm her up before taking her to him. One of the pretty barrel racers was preparing her mount for the upcoming event. Whether Willie wanted to get a better look at the pretty girl or was embarrassed by a race with this short-eared horse, the race was on. When I put the brakes on with the bits and hollered "whoa," she broke into bucking. The bucking stock in this rodeo ought to be ashamed at their performance compared to hers. I would have emptied my pockets to watch the DeMoss boys from my hometown try her that night. My pockets were emptied all right. It was highway robbery with the city slickers frisking a country boy for a high priced ambulance ride to the hospital next door. This major mule wreck put my lights out.

The first thing I remembered after the wreck was very bright lights shining in my face, the kind described by those who have had out-of-body experiences. What really scared me was that there was no beautiful music and that the Man in long flowing white robes was not waiting for me. When I tried to sit up, I could not budge. Thinking I was paralyzed, I let out a war hoop. "Turn me loose,"

I demanded. They had brought me to the hospital on a rigid body board with my head strapped down with Velcro straps. My family and the High Sheriff of Franklin Parish apologized to the hospital staff for my uncharacteristic behavior.

When I was fully awake, I insisted that I be released. To test my mental faculties, they asked me some questions. "What happened?" they asked. I told them that the train ran over me at the crossing on Loop Road. The attendant said, "Sir, they took the tracks up years ago, and no train has been by since." Either I lied, or these guys do not have a penchant for humor. The answers to the next questions revealed which. When were you born? How old are you? What day is it? What color is blue and so forth? I wonder if seventy-five percent is a passing grade on these kinds of tests. They let me go when I signed a consent form that I was crazy and refused medical treatment. My wife and the bigheaded sheriff signed it as witnesses.

On an elk hunt in Colorado, a friend and I had debated on how many board feet of lumber could be sawed from those huge Douglas firs. Leading Willie and Lucy down a mountain trail, I saw a gigantic tree, probably virgin timber, blown down by a windstorm. With all of us standing in the trail, I pointed downhill at the log and said "Look at that lo....' I never got the word log out of my mouth. Willie had a flashback to her former life when a lion ate her. She jumped to a conclusion based on her knowledge of phonics and thought I was going to say "lion" instead of "log" when I pointed. She wheeled around and started to retreat down this trail dragging me on the end of the lead rope. She soon passed the speed limit on the way to the speed of sound with my ricocheting off of saplings, trees, and rocks. So why didn't I try to turn loose? I couldn't with a half hitch around my wrist. After the dust cleared, I assessed the damage. The mules and friend were okay, the rope a bit frayed, and my left knee punished beyond what it was designed to take. I referred to this knee as a gimpy knee when I talked to the orthopedic surgeon who repaired a torn medial meniscus from this second mule wreck.

As I write this line I am in the University of Mississippi Medical Center in Jackson, Mississippi, for a meeting with anesthesiologists, for laboratory blood work, and for appointments with cardiologists and another orthopedic surgeon because I am having surgery tomorrow on my right wrist, a right proximal carpectomy. All of these medical people begin a medical history with the same question, "How did this injury occur?"

"I had a mule wreck," I say, and they begin to look for my sign. I explain that I was legging up the mules for a Colorado elk hunt and acclimating some of my body parts to the contour of the saddle to prevent soreness. I was about two miles from my house when a big English bulldog, a neighbor's family pet, ran to greet us. This dog was ugly and fierce looking. Willie thought right off that it was another lion and that it was going to eat her, not greet her. She went goofy and threw me in the middle of a hard turn row causing another bad wreck with resulting injuries. Two mule wrecks in my life knocked me unconscious, one at the rodeo and one at the turn row. The emergency medical technicians were on the scene when my lights came back on.

The question and answer session was repeated just as the last time. This time I did not care if I had a passing grade or not. That taxi with the big red cross was not going to get anymore of my money. The EMTs had a pretty good sales pitch telling me how bad I looked and how beat up I was, but I thought they ain't going to con me this time. Before they left, they wanted me to admit I was crazy by signing those papers again. According to the clock, my lights were off about twenty-five minutes. "Mattie, Willie is always thinking about lions, and she is apt to break bones when she does. Auto body shops, bone doctors, and ambulance drivers all thrive on wrecks. Mattie, Willie is an accident looking for a place to happen."

Lucy, four years younger than Willie, was born in 1997 to a Tennessee walking mare and a standard jack. She was a just-weaned colt when I first saw her in a pasture about ten miles from my house. She was gangly legged and had to spraddle her legs out to the side to get close enough to the ground to graze. She was so funny looking that she looked like a cartoon character. Kept in a back forty pasture, she was always alone with no pasture buddies. I felt so sorry for her. I went by to check on her two to three times a week, finally stopping after a while to walk out and visit with her. It seemed as if she looked forward to my visits, and she would come to meet me. I always petted her, rubbed her ears, picked up her feet, and scratched her back. Then she would follow me back to the truck and bray as I got ready to leave. I knew she wanted to go home with me, and I went to tell her owner the same. My feathers fell when the man who owned her said he would not part with her. Leaving the gate open, I told him if he ever changed his mind and let me have her, she would have a good home. I continued to see Lucy, and she was always on my wish list. About six months later her owner sent me word that if I still wanted her to come talk to him. He thought she was lonesome because she would bray so loud he could hear her forty acres away. Moving her closer to the house did not stop her cries. Her constant calling reminded him that I would give her a good home and companions to keep her company. "Mattie, Lucy has grown into such a tall graceful lady at 17+ hands."

Copper came here from the neighboring state of Mississippi. Mr. William Morgan of Morgan City, Mississippi, used a Tennessee Walking mare and a standard Jack that was black with white points to produce this beautiful sorrel gaited mule colt, a molly. Mr. Bill Loftin of Delhi, Louisiana, was looking at advertisements in the *Mississippi Market Bulletin* when he saw an ad that blinked at him like a neon sign: gaited mule colts for sale. It did not blink twice before he called and asked if I was interested. He knew that Mary Ann and I were about to celebrate our thirty-fifth wedding anniversary, and he suggested this colt would make a perfect gift for the occasion. The very next Saturday found us at the plantation of Mr. Morgan in the heart of the Mississippi Delta to look at mule colts. A good salesman, Mr. Morgan began to tell us about a flood of people who were looking at and were interested in buying these colts for wives' anniversaries, girl friends' engagements, daughters' Christmas presents, and other special days. With the demand this great and not willing to risk someone else beating us to such a great deal, we immediately put one apiece on lay-a-way.

In the excitement of my good fortune, I never recalled asking Mr. Bill and Mrs. Marilyn Loftin which wedding anniversary they were celebrating since he had also bought a mule colt. Mr. William Morgan gave us a high five, a big smile, and a promise that he would notify us as soon as they were weaned. Two months passed before we got the call to come get the mule colts. This call saved my hide since the anniversary date was two days away. I got a high five, a big smile, and an "attaboy" from Mary Ann when I presented her thirty-fifth anniversary gift. "Mattie, she promptly named her Copper, a fitting handle for this sorrel baby. She is a 2003 model."

Smut came here with a lot of questions. Some questions do not need to be asked in public, some not in private, and some not at all. The best advice may be to let sleeping dogs lie. I have a character flaw, called thinking out loud, and I sometimes need a surgeon to get my foot out of my mouth. Since the Ten Commandments do not list this flaw on the black list, it must not be too bad. Without putting anyone on the spot, no questions will be asked, and thinking out loud will not be allowed. However, a few conclusions have been drawn. This mule must not have been a wedding anniversary present. If this mule were an anniversary present, the advice to let sleeping dogs lie was the rule to abide by. This mule must have left a bad taste in someone's mouth, ruffled a few feathers, and worn out a welcome within five months.

Smut came about five months after Copper, and she was the other colt bought at the same time from Mr. Morgan. She was also an offspring of a Tennessee Walking mare and the black jack. Black as coal, Smut was a beautiful specimen. I visited the Loftin place often to check on her progress in training, which was a bit slow. She seemed skittish and hard to catch. Not many visits came and went until I could get her to take peppermint candy from my hand and rub her from stem to stern. Mr. Loftin wanted to know if I would take her and give her a good home. He sent her licenses, tags, and title paid in full; I assumed that he had sole ownership of Smut since Mrs. Loftin did not co-sign the title. Smut must not have been her anniversary present after all. "Mattie, you have to be careful of the advice of some people. They can cause you to start a fire at your house that you can't put out."

Tensas was born on Mr. William Morgan's plantation in the year 2005, a full brother to Copper and a picture perfect sorrel john mule colt. I placed the order for this colt when I picked Copper up in 2003. The 2004 colt born to her parents was solid black and, because I was looking for a team of sorrels, was rejected. Mr. Morgan called as soon as the next colt's feet hit the ground to see if the deal was still on. I told him I did not back up from many fights, family or otherwise, and that I would send the deposit. I told him to do two things for me: give the ranch hand a high five and a big smile, and take a picture of this colt to send to me. I named this sorrel mule colt after the Tensas River Swamp that afforded so many wonderful memories of my years as a boy growing up. The camping and hunting trips, fishing, and exploring this vast bottomland hardwood forest bring back experiences that money cannot buy. The stories shared around many campfires and the relationships built with other men and their sons have left me richer than I could ever have dreamed. This swamp has been the setting and the scene of many historical events such as the rise of the plantation era when cotton was king, the white gold of the south; the Frisby and Flowers saga of the brick house; the hunting escapades of Theodore Roosevelt, Holt Collier, Ben Lilly and others; the Civil War skirmishes and battles; and the timber industry's impact on the region.

This forest is full of many more stories than I can tell. As the pace of time seems to catch up to me, I am saddened that this place will not do for others what it did for me. Maybe my generation has failed because we have not left the land better than we found it. Nero, the Roman Emperor, was a mad man; however, he said something that has stuck with me. He said, "I found Rome brick, but I have left it marble." It is not how we find things, but rather how we leave them that is important. "Mattie, Copper and Tensas will make a well matched team. I look forward to taking you for a ride in the wagon when they are well broke. I'll tell you some of the stories from the campfires, the experiences with bears, deer, fish, frogs, coons, turkeys, alligators, varmints, pranks, and much more."

Cash and Carri are a pair of sorrel mules that were born on Mr. Bill and Mrs. Marilyn Loftin's place on the banks of Bayou Macon south of Delhi, Louisiana. On February 28, 2007, Mr. Loftin called and asked me to come to his place. Since it seemed urgent, I went quickly. He asked me to get into his truck, and we drove straight to the pasture where several mares and babies were grazing. He asked me to look at the colts to see if anything was wrong. I said, "All of them are deformed except that long-eared one." He began to tell me that this slip up was very embarrassing to him. I told him that these kinds of happenings occur in human families too. The mama of this baby was a high-powered cow horse, a foundation bred quarter horse mare that a young lady from Mississippi placed in the care of Mr. Loftin to breed to one of his top stallions. Mr. Loftin asked me, "What am I going to tell her?" I asked him, "What color hair does she have?" Since the young lady was not blond headed, I told him it might be better to tell her the truth. The very next morning the same thing occurred. I received another phone call that seemed urgent, and I went quickly. Another accident, another sorrel mule colt, stood next to one of Mr. Loftin's prized quarter horse mares. "How many more do you think will show up?" he said. "Time will tell," I said.

Mr. Loftin bought this carousing, promiscuous jack colt along with two Mammoth Jennies and another full-grown Mammoth Jack at the same time I bought Tensas. The young jack colt was turned out with the mares that were to keep him company and baby him. Time can go from plodding along to flying faster than the snap of a finger. In my day, people said you could tell when a boy became a man when he traded his Mickey Mouse wristwatch for a Marilyn Monroe pinup. This chap's interest changed overnight, probably on a moonlight night. Both sorrel colts, one a john and the other a molly, were born a day apart, one on February 28th and the other March 1st, both unplanned.

The young lady from Mississippi sold me the colt born to her mare, and Mr. Bill Loftin gave me the colt born to his mare. Their names became Cash because I bought him and Carri because all I had to do was carry her home. As the clock kept ticking, other mule colts arrived on the Loftin farm, more than enough. The young jack, thought to be too young to reproduce, almost wore out his welcome. He was moved to the mules' by choice pasture where he would bray that song "Don't Fence Me In." This pitiful sound was from such a lonesome soul. "Mattie, I bet these seven mules have eaten two eighteen wheeler loads of peppermint since they have lived here on the farm."

Cinnamon is a registered Missouri Fox Trotting Horse born July 16, 2005, on the farm of Mr. Jim Sullivan of Winnsboro, Louisiana. He and Mrs. Wilma are owners of Sullivan's Feed Store and breeders of Missouri Fox Trotting Horses. Several of these horses have been recognized as world champions. At least two of these horses have been sold overseas to wealthy people of royalty for prices too big for me to calculate. To celebrate the twenty-fifth year of their anniversary in the feed business, Sullivan's awarded a colt as a grand prize. The winner was to be drawn from names of customers who had registered during this period. Mary Ann registered for the drawing in her name, and Mrs. Wilma told her to register for me since I was out of town for a rifle match. The drawing in which my name was chosen very nearly caused a divorce at our house as Mary Ann laid claim to this prize. A real man should not let a woman push him around like she was trying to do me. This conflict is now a legal battle and will likely have to be settled by a judge or jury. To save her the embarrassment of losing in a public arena, I suggested she concede in defeat. I cannot repeat her response at this time or in the future; however, I can reveal that the response was made in a very loud voice. The Sheriff, who is Mary Ann's boss, the assistant district attorney, the Chief Deputy, and many others told her she was fighting a losing battle. Yet she found satisfaction. Satisfaction sometimes comes about through fraud, blackmail, threatening, and other underhanded and illegal means. All these things came out of Mary Ann's mouth, but there were no witnesses present who could testify against her if they came to pass. What really scared me is that a dead man cannot testify. Her claim that she could stack the cards in her favor further troubled me. To make my case in the event of my demise, investigators should look for certain things. If my bed is in the barn, I may have been thrown out of the house. If I am shot, investigators need to ask whether I was shot with the bullet with my name on it or was it an accidental shooting. They need to check whether food poisoning or poisoned food did me in because Mary Ann said it would be easy with my appetite. There is no telling how many good men have died without even an investigation. Medical doctors prescribe Coumadin, a rat poison, as blood thinners for heart patients. If a death occurs and toxicology tests confirm an overdose, they always blame the patient for not following doctor's orders. "Mattie, remember, a dead man cannot testify. Satisfaction may be the best option after all. I think the Bible says something about peacemakers, but I will tell you not to bite the hand that feeds you."

"Mattie, this story about the Rest of the Gang may never end if we don't take up the welcome mat. Have you ever heard of a story too good to be true? Mattie, this woman must think we are two mullets and that she could catch us on the first cast." I smelled a fish all right when Mary Ann started telling us about the next new arrival. It sounded like a cock and bull story to me. This thing just happened to show up one morning when Mary Ann clocked in for work. Even though she is not on the Franklin Parish Sheriff's Office payroll as an investigator, she assumes this role from time to time. She assumed the role this time, but her interpretation of the facts will not hold water under the cross examination of a good defense attorney.

"Mattie, I hope they don't make us raise our right hands and swear to tell the truth because I don't think it would help her case. Mattie, listen to how I remember it." Mary Ann brought her into the bedroom where we were watching television and said, "Look what I found. Somebody threw her away. They probably lost their job and couldn't take care of her, or decided she was too much trouble, or moved to a place that did not allow pets. It's a shame that she was so neglected."

"Mattie Grace, this is how I see it. She did not have one flea, one tick, or one ear mite. She smelled like jasmine and was as fat as a town dog. There is something bad wrong with this picture. Yes, it is a story too good to be true."

This red dachshund female was about six months old and looked like she had just come from a dog show, not off the street. I placed my bets that this was someone's pet that had wandered away from home and that a claim of ownership would come quickly. Advertisement in the local newspaper, *The Franklin Sun*, announcements on KMAR, the local radio station, fliers in businesses, word of mouth, and the veterinarian offices led to no claims of ownership. These efforts ended the investigation, but Mary Ann had better be glad this case never came to trial because circumstantial evidence would surely have convicted her.

I would have loved to put her on the witness stand and said, "Raise your right hand. Do you promise to tell the truth, the whole truth, and nothing but the truth, so help you God?" There are still too many missing pieces to this puzzle for me to have a clear picture of what really happened.

For two weeks these two parlor mates had a good time playing with each other and seemed to be compatible pals. "What are we going to call her?" Mary Ann asked. Watching the new dog move from place to place had started the cogs in my brain turning in the direction of a name. Movies like *Dances with Wolves* excited the Indian blood flowing in my veins. I said to her, "We'll give her an Indian name and call her Wiggles When She Walks."

Mary Ann brought my supper to the bed, a delicious bowl of vegetable soup that I never got to eat. She commented on what an appropriate name this was for our new addition. She wiggled from her nose to the tip of her tail like a snake crawling on the ground. Mary Ann wanted to know how I was so gifted in choosing such a cute and fitting name. It would have been much better if I had lied instead of telling her that Wiggles When She Walks reminded me of my high school girlfriend walking down the hall in school. Live and learn is my philosophy. The next time I am asked such a question, I will invoke the Fifth Amendment and keep my mouth shut. Hot soup can burn a man.

"Mattie, I think Mary Ann thought we had the blinders on when this highfalutin' mutt showed up." Blinders were used on mule bridles to keep them from seeing the whole landscape or all of the surroundings. I bet this mutt had a pedigree that was two feet long. She was high class by this country boy's standard. The proof is in the puddin': pretty is as pretty does. I am impressed by performance dogs, not show dogs. It is hard to eat ribbons and trophies collected at dog shows, but there are a lot of advantages of owning performance dogs that herd sheep and goats; hunt hogs and squirrels; tree bears, coons, and lions; run deer; and serve as seeing eye dogs, dope dogs, bomb sniffers, and many more useful things.

"Mattie, one of the deputy sheriffs who works with Mary Ann said they read the lost ad in the newspaper and heard the radio report that said 'Found: Lost Dog in the vicinity of the Court House. Call to identify'." He overheard a conversation with a caller when Mary Ann asked her the kind and color of the dog she had lost. The lady said that she was a red female dachshund. He said that Mary Ann told the caller this could not be her dog since she was polka dotted. "Mattie, I would love to hook Mary Ann up to a polygraph and interrogate her, but this is the last time you will hear from me on the how, when, and where of Wiggles When She Walks."

Chapter 7

WE ARE FAMILY

Mattie learned that the cast of characters that live in and around this house is very diverse in nature. This place is a virtual zoo that has entertained many people who have come with their children, grandchildren, and friends. The educational opportunities on these guided tours have been eye-openers for both adults and children. A roll call or head count goes something like this: nine cats, five males and four females, all fixed; seven mules, five mollies and two johns; one horse, a mare; sixty plus guineas, of both sexes; chickens of many breeds numbering more than two hundred, about fifty per cent roosters and fifty per cent hens; three dogs, all females and none of which will reproduce.

It is surprising that many people do not know that mules cannot reproduce and have no offspring. Consider the chickens and guineas. The madam of the house was flabbergasted when I told her that the guineas and chickens were not crossbreeding. She then led me to the barnyard to point out a little bantam hen with her brood. She began to give me a lesson on the facts of life, not the birds and bees, but the chickens and the guineas. Her evidence, scratching in the dirt in front of us, consisted of six baby chicks, three baby guineas, and a little hen. Since they were all hatched in the same nest, Mary Ann had come to the conclusion that the little hen had been fooling around with a guinea rooster. We began a lesson in deductive reasoning. Was the hen promiscuous with the guineas or had she stolen these eggs from a guinea nest? Had a guinea laid eggs in her nest perhaps? After my long lecture and persuasive presentation, Mary Ann saw the light about this matter and threatened me if I ever revealed her ignorance of chickens and guineas. I told her that this secret was ours and that getting this story out of me would be harder than stealing gold out of the vault in Fort Knox. As more of these scenes took place, the frequency of mentioning the bullet with my name on it increased. I told Mattie, "Don't smile or giggle when you hear some of these absurd stories that come from Mary Ann. She may just have a bullet with your name on it too. Mercy, I am nervous. The older I get, the more I just nod my head and keep my mouth shut."

Mattie learned that the biggest threat to the harmony and happiness of our family comes from outside influences, and we keep a constant vigil because of a never ending barrage of predators including hawks by day, owls by night, coyotes, foxes, bobcats, bears, wild cats, traveling dogs, coons, skunks, mink, and alligators. In fact, a three-foot long alligator once buried himself in the mud at the northeast corner of the barn. Completely camouflaged, he ate about a dozen baby chicks before I saw a small spot on his head about the size of a quarter and dug him out. He caught a train and went to live just down the road at Big Lake.

"Mattie, the ongoing debate about the balance of nature advocated by wildlife biologists has a lot of merit until we look at the flip side of the coin." This scientific experiment is always ongoing to determine who is right about this debate. The biologists and environmentalists are convinced that man should be taken out of the equation. Then these chicken and guinea bandits and cat and dog-killing thugs could have free range of the farm with no questions asked. I guess these people want me to sit in a rocking chair and twiddle my thumbs while these fearless predators destroy and carry off all of our family. It is true that some hawks and owls die of old age. I have seen evidence from piles of feathers and bones that some have had heart attacks in mid-air and others were so blind they killed themselves by flying into tree limbs at high rates of speed. Some theories are absolute, and others are obsolete. It may take a lifetime to tell who is right in this debate.

The Big Lake Wildlife Management Area and the Tensas River National Wildlife Refuge are contiguous properties owned by the State of Louisiana and the Federal Government. The area boundary begins one mile to the east behind my house. This vast bottomland hardwood forest passed through several owners including Ayres Timber Company, Fisher Lumber Company, Singer Manufacturing Company, Chicago Mill and Lumber Company, and now the State and Federal Governments. My first excursion to hunt and camp in this swamp came in 1947 on the McClain and McIntyre place where Upper Fool River runs into the Tensas River. This excursion was the beginning of a love affair for me that spawned many wonderful memories of campfires, tales, hunts, friendships, and learning experiences that I will never forget.

"Mattie, you would have loved the little tin shack and the old wood stove on the bank of the river which now lie in a heap. The horse pasture and stable are also a casualty." I remember falling asleep with a belly full of fresh roasted peanuts parched on the old wood heater and listening to the winter rains falling on the tin roof. My father, brother, and friends aplenty spent many days and nights here hunting and fishing. I hunted and killed many buck deer, turkey gobblers, squirrels, raccoons and other varmints. Fishing and frogging were equally as good.

The changing of the guard of this land occurred when a change from private ownership to public ownership took place. We can take a perfectly healthy patient, turn him over to the government, and I guarantee it will not be long until we will have to put him on life support to keep him alive. This natural treasure has been ruined because we turned it over to the government. Wildlife managers, wildlife biologists, deer study leaders, timber consultants, and other experts have nearly caused the death of deer hunting on this land. If a cattle farmer applied the government philosophy of raising deer to his cattle operation, he would be out of the cattle business in about three years.

A few years ago I sat on a log and contemplated what had occurred in my lifetime with this pristine work of the Creator. I cried like a baby when I realized that my memories were the only keepsakes I have of this place. Today I offer a challenge that could settle the argument of who is right about game management on this property. The Feds have both a Judd Brake Unit and a Fool River Unit. Each unit could be managed separately. Those who use this resource will ultimately be the judges of who does the best job. Likewise in a similar challenge, the State of Louisiana could do the same with the Big Lake and Buckhorn Units. This issue will never come to a public vote because the powers that be think those of us who use and love the land are too stupid to know what is best.

"Mattie, Mattie, Mattie, listen up!" Twenty-five plus years ago I stood in the pulpit of Lamar Baptist Church and preached a message that I titled "You Ain't seen Nothin' Yet." I predicted changes that would eat at the moral fiber of the American way of life. These changes were legislated and dictated by our elected leaders. We have marched down the wrong road for too long. Fifteen years later, I stood in the same place and delivered a sequel to that message. This one I titled "How Long Will It Be Before You Say Enough is Enough?" Perhaps we have waited too long. The interference and intrusion of the government into the fiber of our society have been so subtle that they have come without much objection from us.

Big Brother has not only told us, but he has also shown us that the right way is wrong and the wrong way is right. I do not believe that the difference between right and wrong is so close that it could warrant a consistent five to four vote on matters that change the course of our lives. The political jostling that takes place in the name of providing a balance of power on the United States Supreme Court is absurd. I did not know there was a balance between right and wrong. The trend by the court has been to bend, change, and mutilate by interpretation the Constitution of the United States of America drafted by our founding fathers. Conservatives and liberals, Republicans and Democrats, the church and the state are still "We the People."

"Mattie Grace, this great nation was born out of the storms of adversity as our forefathers dreamed of life, liberty, and the pursuit of happiness. A republic was fashioned and framed by a constitution that has evolved over time by amendments and ratification to guarantee equality for all. These are those inalienable rights granted by our Creator."

"Mattie, the sacrifice of blood, sweat, and tears should never be taken for granted. The saying 'All gave some, but some gave all' speaks of these sacrifices. Mattie, this land is my home, this is where my heart is, this is my family, and these are my people. As I see it, many changes have hurt our people."

The ruling on *Rowe vs. Wade* has allowed the murder of millions of babies because it is the law of the land. The atrocities of partial birth abortions are accepted with little protest. The use of corporal punishment on one's own children can be against the law. The display of the Ten Commandments and prayer in certain venues is not allowed. The soft position on crime by the justice system has filled our jails with criminals who have more rights than the victims. Displaying a rope in a hangman's noose may be a hate crime, and beating someone to death with a baseball bat may not be. The First Amendment guaranteeing the freedom of speech and the Second Amendment guaranteeing the right to keep and bear arms will always be the targets at the forefront of the fight to bring the average citizen to submission to his government. The major selling point of these new ideas is that the more of our individual rights we are willing to give up, the safer we will all be. "Mattie Grace, these bureaucrats have led us down the wrong path for way too long, and an army of kooks have come to join them."

The Louisiana Black Bear is on the endangered species list. It is a crime to kill one, punishable by jail time and a ten thousand dollar fine, and the guilty one must also replace the bear. Yet the government has approved and supported the killing of fifty million unborn babies by abortion. It seems that Bubba, the southern redneck, likes to kill bears and rock babies and the Feds like to kill babies and rock bears. There is no fine or punishment for killing a baby, and the guilty one does not even have to replace the baby.

Bears and whales, snails and minnows, woodpeckers and hawks, eagles and owls, and many others have brought a host of supporters out of the woodwork. The Hollywood crowd, radio and television personalities, celebrities from other walks of life, and politicians who have sold their souls for votes from special interest groups have formed a coalition of twisted thinkers that want to convert everybody to their persuasion. They think that because we believed in

Santa Claus, the Easter Bunny, and the Tooth Fairy, they can perpetrate another hoax on us, and we would believe it too. These self-described intellectuals think we are the offspring of Bubba, the southern redneck, and as dumb as a post. "Mattie, they have about pushed me as far up in a corner as I am going to go. Enough is enough."

"Mattie, it is awesome how our family functions in harmony with so many personalities and needs." Playmates, roommates, and yard mates seem to be extremely happy and satisfied. I am not sure whether the animals belong to us or we belong to them. Since I pay the taxes, I assume that I own the facilities. I do not recall their ever paying an electric bill, water bill, grocery bill or buying horse feed, scratch grain, cat food, dog food and other treats. The benefits of living in this house with this family outweigh all liabilities; it is an experience that money cannot buy. I told Mattie, "Mary Ann and I are so glad that the Storyteller let us pick you all up. We have been blessed as you have taught us so much. We pledge that we will love you and care for you to the best of our ability. We serve notice to predators, both feathered and furred, that you are off limits to them and that we will protect you at any cost. Mattie, keep your gun cocked. You never can tell when you might need it."

"Mattie, we must sound the alarm bells and alert the rest of the human tribe that we have seen the enemy and it is us. This is how I see it." From our ranks come those who would harm us. The predators of the world, the devil's bunch, have opened season on the human family with dire circumstances permeating all of society. The lack of a moral compass in the lives of parents has translated into the lives of young people who are adrift with no direction or purpose. We need to revive our parental responsibility and renew the watch over our families. The place to curb crime is in the high chair, not in the electric chair. If we do not correct our children, the Department of Corrections will. The little bantam hens in the yard with their brood will puff up their feathers to look fierce because they willingly defend their young at all cost, even with their lives. Rottweilers, pit bulls, and all other comers do not excite any fear in these little hens that will attack without any reservation. The assault on the traditional family is relentless and never ending. It is a multi-faceted tactic that seems to come from the pits of hell. Divorce is common. We speak the vows of marriage with little conviction anymore, and "until death do us part" is disregarded. Dysfunctional families reside at sixty-plus percent of the addresses in this country. "His children, her children, and our children" is the norm for most families in this day and age. Evidence of an eroding belief in family values, single parent homes represent far too great a segment of society.

"Mattie you know how much I love you and how I promised to take care of you. Nurturing and loving children must also come from fathers and mothers who have a deep commitment to each other and who build on foundational principles taught in the Word of God. Mattie, this is the way, or I am confused. I think people ought at least to try God's way." One of the greatest responsibilities of parenthood is learning how to discipline one's children. Respect is earned and taught by example. We must be what we want them to become. The role of the parents is to build fences and establish boundaries that will allow the healthy development of their children. The very first thing that will happen is that children will test the fence. The hardest word in any language is no. Discipline at home is reflected in self-discipline at school and healthy development in other areas of life.

Education is a very valuable ingredient that is necessary to personal growth. I told Mattie that lessons learned from the School of Hard Knocks and those learned from a more formal school are equally important. Some information soaks in more quickly than other information. The most effective environment for intellectual growth is created when schools and teachers are the facilitators for learning and parents reinforce learning by demanding an effort on the part of their children. Support and discipline on both ends of the spectrum are requirements for success. Assigning blame and shame will never settle the rift about who is at fault for a disgusting failure to educate many of our children. We must join heads, hearts, and hands to provide the best learning opportunities for America's most valuable resource, our children. If we do less, we have failed.

Members of the average family need to learn that life is not a lottery or a game of chance; therefore, each person should set goals. A systematic plan of action will help us reach these goals. To avoid the many detours on the road of life, one must look, listen, and heed the warnings of others who have traveled on this journey. The experimental use of drugs and alcohol is dangerous and leads to a dead end pursuit. Peer pressure and the thirst for popularity have caused many young people to explore the avenue of sexual freedom that actually enslaves them in unwanted pregnancies and parenthood. Many of the decisions we make follow us to the grave, and other decisions can take us there. It is sad to say that I have stood with grieving parents at the graves of several young people who had no second chance from a decision that could not be erased.

I pointed out to Mattie that the gadget-addicted now generation has thrown common sense out of the window in the over indulgence and use of these gadgets. The cell phones, iPhones, iPads, iPods, Twitter, Facebook, My Space, computers, and other inventions hamper performance in the workplace, the classroom, threaten safety on the highway, and cost a fortune in fees and lost production. If we open our eyes, we can see for ourselves. We see clerks on cell phones, not the phones for business, people driving down the road often texting, not talking, and the young and old alike with a cell phone in their pockets. We may find one half of the employees on a cell phone at their jobs. The vices and abuses and the lack of common sense negate many of the advantages of the technological age. In my opinion, there would be much less distraction in the workplace and classroom if these things had never come on the scene. A drunken driver and a texting driver are equally as dangerous. It is all right with me if we hang them both. It may be necessary to limit the use of these gadgets on the highway, at the workplace, and in the classroom. People should give full attention to the tasks at hand. The Internet has fed perversions of all kinds: pornography, pedophilia, sexual fantasies, and extramarital affairs. These addictions and cravings have wrecked many lives and marriages, and the family is often wounded beyond repair.

"Mattie, Mattie, Mattie, look up! Help for our family is from above."

Chapter 8

HEALING FROM THE INSIDE

As I prepared to turn the light out for a night of sleep, I looked at the little ball of fur on the pillow next to mine. I thought of how frail, weak, hungry, naked, and sick she was the first time I saw her, and now forty-five days later she was a new creature. I visited her every day during her isolation and assured her that this ordeal of dipping and scrapings would rid her of the misery and suffering she had endured from the mange. The gang who lives here welcomed her without objection. She came here house broken. Her letting me know when she needed to take a walk outside was a trait I attributed to her intelligence. She spent every moment the last two weeks, every day and night, in my presence. Friends and strangers alike thought I was a basket case and wondered when I might be admitted to the funny farm for taking in such a mangy mutt. When I told them it was a God Thing that happened on the side of the road, the expressions on their faces were priceless. Some people do not have a clue about God Things; others understand perfectly. I turned the light out, reached over, touched her and said, "Good night, Mattie Grace, I love you." Little snoring sounds quickly put me to sleep.

The live alarm clock, Little Man, sounded the beginning of a new day from the great room. Mattie responded with two sharp barks to let the rest of the family know that we are up and at 'em. Her behavior was comical as she made sure that I would include her in the day's activities. She followed me every step until I headed towards the door, but she always beat me there to lead me out. It was hard to believe that Mattie was the same creature that came from the thicket; the one who was so elusive and ran from me now ran to me. She quit listening to her head and listened to her heart. All healing comes from the inside out.

My father moved to this small farming community in the fall of 1942 to teach agriculture. Part of the culture of the people who lived here was that it afforded some of the best hunting and fishing found anywhere. Doctor Cincinnatus Dixon Powell provided medical care for the inhabitants of Crowville, Louisiana, and the surrounding area. A legend in his time, he was an icon who was humorous and fun-loving. Many stories were told by him and about him. The agriculture teacher and the country doctor visited the lakes, rivers, and woods at every available opportunity as partners in crime. If people listened to their stories, they always caught too much or killed too much, or else they lied about their exploits.

After one of these trips, Dad told a story I will never forget. After a Saturday morning of fishing, he and Dr. Powell arrived back at the drugstore to find a man sitting on a bench on the front porch with a fish bait stuck to his nose. Through the little wire-rimmed glasses perched on his nose, Dr. Powell inspected the situation. He said to the man, "Looks like you are in a heck of a mess to me." This patient held a nine hook Lucky Thirteen in his hand with a treble hook stuck completely through one nostril.

Dr. C. D. Powell turned to his long time trusted nurse, Mrs. Winnie Dotson, and said, "He needs a tetanus shot. I'll be back." The man did not speak directly to the doctor. In a voice loud enough for the doctor to hear, he asked the nurse if he was going to get this thing taken out of his nose. The man must have thought that the tetanus shot was to be the only plan of action. Doc walked away and said, "I've got a box full of fish I have to skin." He said to Dad, "Don't leave, Ag, I may need some help." He did not say whether the help was needed to skin the fish or to get the bait out of the man's nose. This kind of humor will get you a cussing most of the time, but it can also get you killed.

After washing and attending to personal hygiene, the doctor started to tend to the business of extracting the hook from the man's nose. Mrs. Winnie drew up a large syringe of Novocain to use as a local anesthetic to deaden the tissue around the hook. Dr. Powell asked the man to turn the bait over to him. This was not a good request because pain was about to commence. Doc began to inject the anesthetic into the man's nose while pulling on the bait. As tears ran down the man's cheeks and dripped off his chin to the floor, my Dad yelled "Whoa" as though he were talking to a mule. Dad entered this fray to offer advice to the doctor and stop the pain for this poor man. The barb of the hook was in clear sight at the bottom of the nostril, and Dad suggested that the doctor cut the barb off and just slip it out. Doc picked up a scalpel and began to cut tissue on the surface of the nose where the hook went in, and he said he did not want to ruin such a good Lucky Thirteen.

Nothing else was said, all parties left, but each had questions and opinions about the other. My father later said he did not sleep that night because he was thinking about the pain the doctor needlessly inflicted on this poor man. An educated man, a doctor, was so stupid as to ignore advice on the best way to remove the hook. As Dad stopped at the post office to get the mail the next day, Dr. Powell walked to the front porch of the drugstore and asked him to come drink coffee. He said, "Collier, about that hook in the man's nose yesterday. That was a puncture wound, and the likelihood of an infection is much greater with a puncture than an open wound. If a puncture closes first on the outside, the infection is trapped internally; and it will continue to grow. If infection had developed, it would have made an ugly hole, and skin grafts would be the only means of repair. Since the bait had been fished in dirty water and had hung many fish with germs, the risk of infection increased. It was necessary for me to debride the flesh around the hook and open it up so that it could heal from the inside out."

"Why didn't you tell me yesterday, so I could have slept last night?" Dad asked.

"Because you yelled 'Whoa' too loud, " the doctor said. When tempers flare, it is best to leave well enough alone until they cool off. A big shot lawyer from the neighboring Town of Winnsboro, Louisiana, had paid the injured man a day's wages to paddle the boat so that the lawyer could bass fish in Indian Lake and Lick Bayou.

Equipped with the finest gear, a Pflueger Supreme Reel, custom bamboo rod, and a box full of bait, the lawyer began his day at first light. In the practice of law there are some things an attorney must learn to do and some things he must learn not to do. In fishing, a fisherman must also learn some things to do and some things not to do.

The first rule in bass fishing instructs the fisherman not to cast up or down the plane of the boat as bad things can happen. The hired man was not paid enough for what happened next. He was impressed by the good gear of the lawyer, but he was unimpressed by how the lawyer used the gear. A bass struck a shad near a cypress knee in front of the bow of the boat. Because of the low-pressure area between the lawyer's ears, he forgot rule number one. As he made the backswing, a rod that was too long and a boat that was not long enough resulted in rule one being broken. As the hook sank into the guide's nose, the rod immediately started forward. The lawyer knew that something was wrong when the other man ran all the way from the back of the boat to the front. A backlash as big as a wasp's nest filled the spool of the reel. The attorney apologized, and the two fishermen reviewed the rules all the way to the doctor's office. The lawyer dropped the injured man off at the drugstore to wait for the doctor and said that he had to go get a drink to calm his nerves. The lawyer was later elected as a judge, but he did not get this hooked man's vote. Dr. Powell told this story, and he said he would have liked to measure this man's temper instead of his temperature. The man was sore in the nose and hot in the collar.

Mattie began to remind me of roses in the springtime—first bare and naked, then leaves coaxed by the warm rays of the sun bringing a birth of buds, and finally blooming bouquets of flowers bathed in fresh fragrances. These things are God Things just like Mattie's transformation. The phenomenon of changing seasons and changed lives is explained in the expression of faith that simply says, "I believe." Apart from faith, the interpretation of life would lead us down a dead-end street to a foolish conclusion. If we ever embrace the idea that He is the Potter and we are the clay, this affirmation will change the dynamics of our lives. Healing always comes from the inside out.

There was so much of Mattie's life that I wanted to know about if only she could talk. Where did she come from? Who brought her here? Why did they throw her away? What did she think about the tin-top house? Had she ever dreamed of a place like her new home? It was probably much better that I did not know the answers to many of these questions because I then would inquire about names, addresses, and directions. People that can treat one of God's creatures this way ought not take up the good air that a possum could breathe. Where these people are concerned, if it came down to a possum or people vote, they could not politic me hard enough to get my vote.

Mattie never took those big brown eyes off of me, constantly watching my every move, waiting for a tap on my thighs as her invitation to come sit in my lap. She jumped with such enthusiasm that it looked as if she could jump over the house. Like the flags of friendship, her ears and tail flapped and wagged in the breeze. The love stories of Anthony and Cleopatra, Romeo and Juliet, and Cinderella and Prince Charming pale in comparison to this story that began in such unlikely circumstances.

I talked to Mattie as though she were educated at Harvard, Yale, Georgetown, or some other prestigious university that conferred advanced degrees. It was very hard to distinguish sometimes who was the teacher and who was the student. Was I a reflection of her, or was she a reflection of me? The mutual language of love was spoken between us with expressions that could never be counterfeited. White washing the pump house does not change the water in the well, so whatever is down in the well still comes up in the bucket. Mattie overflowed with exuberance and enthusiasm like an artesian well. The changing of the water in the well is in itself a God Thing. The fuel that fired her heart was gratitude from deep within her soul. As I watched this healing that came from her heart, I too was grateful for the work of grace. Why would anyone want to pick us up?

Helping a person understand grace is an impossible task. The concept is too deep for any of us to fathom and define. A pen does not hold enough ink to explain grace, yet it is small enough to be embraced by the heart. Grace is not a head thing; it is a heart thing.

Not until someone experiences some God Things will he understand about grace. Many people already know. They have been blessed!

God Things are a matter of grace designed by the Grand Architect of Life. The same One who gives color to the rainbows also flavors those lives who desire to taste Him. My first taste at the Homochitto River forty-five years ago was the first of many experiences that can be explained only by grace. The events of the few weeks that began at the thicket on the river where I found Mattie and led to the dramatic change in her life were all God Things that come under the heading of matters of grace.

The experiences of grace are like snowflakes. Each one is different from the other by design. Mattie Grace and I experienced a matter that can only be embraced by the heart—a God Thing. Nothing but trash to one man and thrown away, Mattie lived as my treasure. Sometimes the best of treasures emerges from a trash pile.

The two of us became an inseparable duo, constant companions linked together by a third party whose presence magnified the moment. The jokes, the needling, the snide remarks, and the insinuations of a deficiency of my mental faculties followed us everywhere we went. I heard comments like "Where did you get such an ugly dog? Man, that mule must have hurt your thinker when she threw you to make you want that mangy mutt. Horrors, what is that thing following you?" This constant barrage of questions came from a bunch of folks who put their mouths in gear before shaking the rocks around in their brains and getting them into the right slots to think.

"Mattie, if they only knew the whole story." This matter of grace story between Mattie and me compelled me to share with the naysayers and others who would listen about her life. I told her, "Mattie, just look at the source of this ridicule. The only thing they have following them is jealousy because they do not have a friend like you to follow them. Mattie, I don't know of a dog who would not be embarrassed to be seen with them." Snide remarks and teasing comments soon turned to envy as everyone watched this one who was so near death become so full of life. Mattie's heart was like a well with healing waters that bathed her from the inside out. Both Mattie and I walked away from our pasts grateful for the bridge that led to a new life. This life became the story that we must share. It was a Matter of Grace.

Jesus, the Storyteller who told the story of the Good Samaritan, used an earthly story in a temporal setting, a masterpiece in simple language, to express a truth of divine dimensions. In my lifetime, I have had many assignments, some welcomed and some not, but none so compelling to me as telling the story about Mattie and me. Since I do not have the ability or capability to express in words the true meaning of the whole story, I have depended on the Salt of the Earth to flavor it and the Light of the World to illuminate it for others to read.

People say we cannot judge a book by the cover. When we judge someone by what we see on the outside, we often act as Passer Uppers and not Picker Uppers. Over time, and especially when I told people the Matter of Grace story, no one laughed anymore when they saw Mattie and me. As everyone saw the remarkable changes that took place, other opinions about the true value and beauty of her life emerged. Mattie Grace became a real-life walking sermon, one that was seen and not said. Many people would rather see a sermon any day than hear one because a living sermon usually lasts longer.

This little junkyard dog enriched my life and increased my worth. She became the Picker Upper in this old man's life. If I were a cake, I would be a plain one. Mattie came to put the icing on this old man's cake.

Chapter 9

THE PREACHER

Watching Mattie Grace grow was like watching a sermon grow. I would rather see a sermon any day than hear one. She became well known in our community as word of her rescue spread, and she was willing to be seen with me. She went with me everywhere I went: to the barbershop, to my work, to my friends, to nursing homes, to the feed store, to the courthouse, to the bank, to the sheriff's office, to the coffee shop—everywhere. It seemed that she was always the center of attention and people sometimes asked her, "Mattie, what is that following you?"

Sometimes in some churches puppets are more popular than the preacher. It dawned on me that if a puppet could tell a story, so could a mutt. She agreed that I would be the dummy and that she would be the ventriloquist and tell me what to say. I am glad that she picked me, and it was such an honor for me to help her tell her story. My life was forever changed by her life. Mattie was unashamed about her love and devotion to me, a passion so strong that she would give her life to defend me. As word of her life spread, people constantly provoked her to respond in protecting me. If someone got between us, she would fuss and growl. If they jerked on my pants legs, she pulled furiously on theirs. Her intelligence told her this provoking was all in fun, but the more intense the fun, the more fierce the response. Mattie Grace had such a magnetic personality that people were naturally drawn to her. How to win friends and influence people were qualities born when she experienced the healing from the inside. The best was yet to come.

Mattie, even though a dog, joined the ranks of all who minister in spiritual things. There are no stereotypes for those God calls. No one size fits all, and there are no unique qualities that are common to all. The people who serve come from all walks and occupations of life. If we were going to draft a team of winners, many of those selected would not have made the team. Many fumbled the ball and caused the team to be penalized, hindering instead of helping. How could a bunch of sheep and goat herders, fishermen, carpenters, tax collectors, bellyachers, and hard headed, unpolished people be molded into a winning team? The ones sitting on the sidelines were always making snide remarks and jokes, often cheering when one of these made a mistake. It is remarkable how He takes a bunch of misfits, also-rans, cripples, leftovers, weaklings, and common people to do such an impossible task. If and when they fail, He just picks them up, dusts them off, and puts them back into the game. If He took everyone that failed out of the game, there would be no one left at the end. I have seen men hurt, injured, fatigued, and discouraged who took themselves out of the lineup. We need to encourage those who lead us on the spiritual journey of faith. They sacrifice to make our way easier and our response often discourages them. Every team needs its cheerleaders. Mattie and I became a team with me cheering her on every step of the way.

The common thread that ties those who minister in spiritual things is the feeling that their marching orders come from the same place. There is a deep conviction by the "called" and the "chosen" that a divine encounter moves one to respond without reservation, even though it is often met with reluctance. This reluctance may be perceived to be on the order of pulling teeth, but without the benefit of a painkiller.

The ministry of messengers was followed like a footprint through both the Old and New Testaments. God passed along instructions from His spokesmen to His people on their journey from the beginning to the end. If there is a handbook or specific plan and instructions on how to carry out these orders, I have not received mine yet. The trail may be a bit dim at the beginning and shrouded in mystery, but it becomes clearer as this journey moves toward the destination. The pioneers of the journey were the patriarchs like Abraham, Isaac, and Jacob who were the lighthouses along the way in the early days of the trip. Moses' divine encounter with the burning bush in the desert prepared him to receive the first instructions from the Designer of the journey. As he stood barefoot in this Holy Place, his reluctance was measured by his response. Moses was afraid none would believe him and that there was someone else more qualified. The signature on all of the marching orders was signed, "I Am hath sent you." The voices of the patriarchs were meant to give direction to a wandering people on their way to a promised land. God began to prepare a people for this prepared place. Moses' task of judging the people was so monumental that others came to assist in providing direction to them. The man Moses delivered the Tablets of the Law from Mount Sinai as an edict from the Lawgiver.

As more people joined the journey and the numbers increased, a greater demand for those who labored in spiritual things multiplied. The pilgrimage from the bondage in Egypt was an enormous undertaking with more than one and one-half million men, women, and children, along with their flocks and herds, beginning this trek in the wilderness. The disobedience of a rebellious people often found them on a detour instead of on the main road. As we follow their footprints, it is as though they were sheep without a shepherd. Forty years of frustration and blame by a people that did not hear and heed the voices crying in the wilderness was a very high price to pay.

The promises of a land called Canaan and a place called Heaven tell us how to get there and how to live there. The record of the people is found in the journals of the Scriptures. The ministry of the Word, once shrouded in mystery, is becoming clearer as we move along. So that the blind would not be leading the blind, God set aside certain men and a certain tribe to give direction and counsel to this people: some patriarchs, some priests, some prophets, some to preach, and some to pastor. These men came from all walks and occupations of life and faced the same struggles and conflicts as the people they led. There was not a man among them that was perfect! With Mattie, it seems He used a small dog to influence people.

The chronicles of the Scripture are a truthful account of the good, the bad, and the ugly in the lives of these men. No cover up existed; the stories were told just as they occurred. These imperfections, as in all men, have set the stage for ridicule. Other occupations, organizations, and associations have been the targets of ridicule and jokes also. The three leaders at the brunt of these jokes are preachers, lawyers, and Texas Aggies.

Ecclesiastical and theological boundaries were enlarged and tied to the doctrine of the priesthood of all believers. A new dimension of ministry that joined both the old and the new Covenants developed. The role and doctrine of preaching became central to the spreading of the Gospel to all the world. Only those who have felt a special summons to this call to preaching can speak with assurance and authority about what they experienced. Jesus gave us a model to follow as he led the way by example, by preaching, by teaching, and by healing.

Those who minister in the word wear many hats and carry many titles whose listing is never exhausted: the Pope, Cardinal, Monsignor, minister, preacher, prophet, priest, pastor, brother, doctor, teacher, reverend, Rev, Right Reverend, bishop, elder, steward, deacon, rabbi, and evangelist. How these titles are dispensed or dispersed is not at all clear to me. The assignment of titles seems to have some degree of sophistication. These may be educational, denominational, financial, political, or some other criteria. In the awarding of doctoral degrees, some are earned and some are learned. The ones who wear the title of doctor often expect an attachment of sophistication. The denomination I am familiar with bestows degrees of doctor on people who raise the most money for its universities or children's homes. Some schools will award this degree for a certain fee, a mail order type. Often a leader in church growth receives an honorary doctorate as a reward. In these ways some degrees are earned. The learned degrees are the heavyweights in academic circles and should be research degrees if they carry the title doctor. Someone said, "Preaching is a gift to be exercised, not an art to be learned." No truer words have ever been spoken.

How leaders in other denominations and some of my preacher friends received their titles is a subject I know little about. When I asked some of them how their titles came about, they did not give me a clear explanation. I asked one who was an elder if he received his title when he got his AARP card. He just laughed. Through an announcement in the local newspaper, one of my favorite preachers was called a bishop. His people were honoring him for years of faithful service and were showing their love for him. No one I knew had heard him called bishop before this time. We were proud for him. I told the barber shop crowd that his church probably had led the state in the selling of peanut brittle for a year and that the title of bishop was a reward and to spread the word. He was not proud of us.

There has been a growing concern about the number of men who are answering the call to the ministry. As the need increases, it seems that the numbers are dwindling. To soothe the pain, I tell my preacher friends that it was easier for men to hear the call when plowing a mule or dragging a cotton sack picking cotton and that one could hear a lot more clearly with sweat running down his face or with calluses on his hands. Joking about preachers may be close to the truth.

When Brother Mack Walker from Jonesville, Louisiana, the pastor at Larto Baptist Church, asked me to preach a revival at the church, Mattie went with me each night and slept in the car while I preached. Then she joined us for food and fellowship at the conclusion of each service. She was a part of our team. Young and old alike were mesmerized by her effervescent and vivacious personality and wanted to know more about the story that brought us together. When I told them I found her in a trash pile, the questions always got more intense and direct. Brother Mack suggested that she tell her story the last night of the revival so that everyone could hear. The place was packed in anticipation of the rest of the story. I was so proud of her as I held her in my arms to tell her story. She told it sincerely.

Mattie's Story

My life changed the day my mama died. She was so weak and sick from nursing six babies. The mange that ravaged her body was passed to all of us. As she grew cold in death, I thought of her sacrifice for us. She had to scrounge for her food for strength to nurse us.

My mama's master had enough money to buy whiskey, tobacco, and cigarettes but would not spend one red cent to feed her. A man that will feed the habits that can kill him and neglect a poor mother and her babies makes no sense to me.

Last night two of my brothers and two of my sisters died. Nobody but me and Tater are left, and we miss mama so much. We moved closer to the house and drank water trapped in an old tire, but our cries for food went unanswered. Later that day the mean old man came out of the house, screamed at us, and chased us back toward the barn. He didn't want the sight he saw to haunt him any longer. These memories must be hauled away. He threw my mama, two brothers, and two sisters, and me and Tater into the back of the truck for the trip to the thicket by the river.

My mother's, brothers', and sisters' sufferings were now over, but mine and Tater's had just begun. As he threw mama and the babies behind the concrete barricades to rot, I thought about how cruel life can be. I remembered the sound of the truck as it went out of hearing. There must have been two hundred vehicles that passed us as we sat there those last two days, but no sound of the one who left us. I understand now what someone means when they say some things are worse than dying. The hunger from the lack of food may make death the easy way out.

As we sat side by side on the abandoned roadway, a truck came around the curve and began to stop. A man called out for us to stop as we ran into the thicket. The more he called, the farther we went. When he had left, we sat in our usual place. A short time later the truck rapidly drove onto the old abandoned roadway, the man jumped out with a gun in his hand, and we barely escaped. Forty-five minutes passed before I raked up enough courage to look him in the eye. He lowered the gun as if he had had a change of heart. Could I trust those eyes?

The truck and the man left and soon returned with an abundance of food that he left in a bowl on the old roadway. We ate more than enough, and much more was left in the bowl. The old stove that was discarded as junk in the wash became our shelter from the weather. The stench that burned my nose came from the rotting flesh of my mother, brothers, and sisters and seared an indelible memory in my heart. I loved my mama!

We recognized the sound of the truck that brought our food. It had been two days since it had been here. The man got out with food and treats in hand, a bag of dog food, and plenty of water, wanting and inviting us to come closer. When we refused, he threw several pieces for each of us and then drove off after leaving the bowls full of food and water.

Mange is such a horrible disease, a miserable existence, tolerated by constant scratching, licking, and gnawing at open sores. Wallowing in the mud at the spring near the river gave some temporary relief, but it must be often repeated. Tater thought the man wanted to be our friend, but I reminded him of what had happened to our mother and siblings. There was no reason why anyone in his right mind would have any interest in us I told him.

It was a cat and mouse game with the outcome unsure. Tater howled most of the night when he got caught in the live trap, and I felt sorry for him when the two men took him away the next morning. Two days later in the shadows of darkness I thought I could steal enough food out of the trap to satisfy my hunger. I had not eaten in two days. As the door snapped shut, I willingly surrendered my all to the one who would come for me.

The drape was raised on my cage, and the new day brought a new beginning in my life. The first words out of this man's mouth were "I won't hurt you, I love you. This is a matter of grace, Miss Mattie Grace." He took me to a big tin top house and bathed me in warm water, careful not to hurt my sores. He said it was necessary to prepare me for a trip to the veterinary office where I would be reunited with Tater.

He told me that the mange I had was much like leprosy. Namaan the leper dipped seven times in the Jordan River to be healed, and my healing would come after I was dipped until clean. Tater and I had to stay in our own pet carriers in the utility room because of the risk of infecting the other pets. We went back and forth to the vet's office every seven to ten days for scrapings and dipping. The man and his wife visited us and told us several times a day that it would soon be over.

We never dreamed that life could be so good. Tater finished his treatments before me and was excited he was going to live with a loving family. We promised we would see each other again, a promise we kept many times.

The man who opened the door to the utility room said, "Mattie, it is over, you are clean." He opened the door of the pet carrier and picked me up again to cradle me in his arms.

"You will not have to stay here again, I promise." As we climbed the stairs he told me that I had to be washed all over like Peter to stay in the big house.

I certainly didn't mind and willingly welcomed this washing. The soothing suds and the warm winds of the hair dryer felt so good that the miserable memories of mange began to fade. Memories of my mother and her sacrifice will always live with me. She probably died thinking she had failed. I said, "Mama, I will always love you."

The man who is now my master laid me on a pillow next to him and said, "Good night, Mattie Grace, I love you." The pillow soaked up the tears of sorrow and the tears of joy that I cried.

I pinch myself every morning to make sure that I am not dreaming because it seems these things are too good to be true. It makes no sense to me why this man would take us in. I hear other people talk behind his back, and they think his brain tumors may have affected his thinking. These same people say that he has had this problem from early childhood, so the tumors may not be the cause. Everyone knows he is nearly deaf, and now they think he may be going blind. He looks at me and says, "Mattie, you are getting so pretty. I love you so much!" The veterinarians tell us that we ought to be thankful for the man who brought us to this place of healing because we were so close to death. They said he literally captured us from the grave. One of the little girls who worked there said it reminded her of ten lepers who were healed of their leprosy and that only one came back to thank the One who was responsible for his healing. There is so much about this man I can't explain. He is so different, but I want to know more. I wish there were something I could do especially for him.

Not only was he so different, but those who lived in the big tin top house seemed to be one big family. No one would want to run away if every door and window were thrown wide open. In fact, I don't think anyone could take a big stick and run them away from there. The first time he carried me up the stairs to the living area, he put me on the floor and said, "Look around and see what you think." I have never wanted to run away. Everyone seems happy, satisfied, and content to live there. He said, "Mattie, I hope you will enjoy your stay here and that you will have a lot of fun."

My master talks to me just like I am his best friend. He talks to me as if these things are a reflection of his heart. I enjoy living at the big house, but he says we won't live here forever because one day we are going to the really Big House. Nearly every day when we pass by a house, he will say, "I had two friends who lived there, but they are now at the really Big House." We went to the Crowville Masonic Cemetery to put a bouquet of flowers on a grave, and he told me this man was his best friend—this man was his father. He hung his head in silence for a long time then looked at me and said, "Mattie I will see him one day at the Big House." We walked all over the cemetery reading the epitaphs on the tombstones. It was like walking through a garden of memories. These memories were keepsakes etched deeper than the epitaphs chiseled in stone. He remarked over and over how each one had contributed to his life and how grateful he was. These were tender moments.

Everyday I spend with him is like an adventure with something new around every corner, people, places, and things to entertain me. He told me the other day why he stayed in such a hurry. Everyone talks about how fast he drives. He said he was driving down the road awhile back at a high rate of speed when he looked in the rearview mirror and a cloud of dust was getting closer. He slowed down to see who it was, and it was Father Time. He has been in a hurry ever since. "Mattie," he said, "Father Time will slip up and put his hand on us one day." I think he tries to cram so much living into each day because he thinks his time is running out. Talking about the Big House and going there seems always to be on his mind. I will tell everyone to keep his suitcase packed because he does not know when we will leave.

As Mattie spoke, a Holy hush, a quiet that was nearly eerie, invaded the church as each person listened to her story. She made it clear that this was not a story about a man and dog, but that it was a story about a God Thing that happened to a man and a dog. There was not a dry eye in the house when she finished.

We adjourned to the fellowship hall for the evening meal. A host of people, the young and the old, came to pet her, hold her, love on her, and compliment and comment about her life. Several of my preacher friends who were visiting at this service said I needed to take some lessons from her. These preachers were all heavyweights with fancy titles laughing at me, a lightweight, who needed some polish. They said that I was like the cross-eyed discus thrower who would never set any records but that I was good at keeping the crowd awake. I knew Mattie had some preacher blood in her veins when I saw her affinity for chicken each night at supper after church. I cleared my throat, and in a loud voice I said, "Mattie Grace, you better watch how much chicken you eat or you will have one of those chicken graveyards hanging over your belt like some folks I know." Everybody hee-hawed except those fat cat preachers. She slept in my lap all the way home, both of us tired and drained from a long week.

There are a few observations that I have made about preachers. Preaching is almost always preceded by the passing of the hat or the taking of an offering. If a preacher tells you to send your money and gifts to God, why does he always tell you to send it to his address? Many of my preacher buddies put clergy signs on their cars. They say it benefits them when parking at hospitals, nursing homes, and other places. I tell them that if I had a clergy sign on my car, people would let the air out of my tires. They too would be victims if they let the hammer down when they preached. Many preachers put their clergy pins on their lapels when they go to buy a new suit. I had just as soon get a tin cup and beg for mine. I have never heard a heavyweight preacher talk about sending too many chickens to the chicken graveyards that hang over their belts or call for a fast in their churches. The subject of gluttony is never ever mentioned. A lot of sins are easier to hide than being grossly overweight, and preachers may be inclined to expose the hidden sins. There is a tendency to lump all who minister together, and often the entire group has a black eye or bad reputation because of a few bad eggs.

A door of opportunity always opened when someone asked how Mattie Grace got her name. It is strange for a dog to have a front name and a back name unless they are of the pedigreed pure blood variety. However, her fame spread far and near, and those who had heard her story either passed it along or wanted me to share it with their friends. It was at the barbershop, the one where I wrote "highway robbery and a bunch of thieves" on the public notice when haircuts went up from $10.00 to $12.00, that I shared the amazing, a matter of grace story, on a Saturday morning with a group of men. The Reverend Virgil "Bo" Harris, the Bishop of Gilbert, was present and soaked up, like a sponge, the particulars that took place at the thicket by the river. The story of the old man and the abandoned dog strummed on the strings of the heart. Deep chords of sympathy made music for the soul.

The local radio station, KMAR, provides time of inspiration and devotion to its listeners. After one of these broadcasts several people called and reported that Mattie's story had been told by the Reverend Harris or Bishop Bo on the morning program. I had rather refer to him as my friend Brother "Bo" Harris than by titles more formal. He tells me he has used her story to talk about the second chances that are offered to dogs and people when we are willing to be used as Picker Uppers. Because so many treasures are found in trash piles, we must always look for them. Preaching is not about getting people out of the slums, but rather about getting the slums out of people, and not just getting us to Heaven, but rather getting Heaven into us.

Chapter 10

LET'S RUN AND PLAY

Almost everyone I know lives life in the fast lane, but sometimes life is like a cat eating a grindstone. It is slow, slow getting it done, but it can be done, only it is tough on the teeth. There is a lot of wear and tear in life. It seems that the older we get, the slower we get. Pairing Mattie Grace and me at this stage in life is like putting a seventy-year-old man in the thirty-year-old group of runners in the Boston marathon. The only thing that this lineup accomplishes is that the old man gets to eat a lot of dust. I am at the place in life where I am counting the sunsets, not planning on the next race.

I told Mattie that whittling on a stick or cutting too many hay strings would dull a knife. I subscribe to the expression that "all work and no play make Jack a dull boy!" We would always look for things to do to sharpen our lives. I promised her that we would have fun when she came to live here and to keep her knife sharp. All I had to do was say, "Mattie, it's a beautiful day to run and play." She would look like she had a shot of adrenaline. Excitement and enthusiasm, like children promised a walk in the park or a trip to the zoo or to pick blackberries, made her hyper with expectation.

Mattie was faster than fast. I think Daniel Webster would have said she was "sudden." Sudden is about the same speed as greased lightning. Sudden is pretty swift for a country boy or an astronaut. It is fast enough to make an old man pull a hamstring. Old men and young dogs all have to run at their own pace. Only one has to decide that winning is not important, and I forgot which one. The injury to Mattie's right back leg when she was a pup left her with a noticeable limp at a walk. It was never a hindrance, not even detected, when she ran.

Three dogs in one household will eventually lead to the establishment of a pecking order. A pecking order is the ranking among horses, mules, dogs, cats, chickens, and guineas. I was about to say with husbands and wives too when my memory slipped me, but the rolling pin helped my recall of who was at the top of the order. Meg reminded us of a sumo wrestler, built for strength and not for speed. Her self-esteem comes not from winning foot races, but from eating another bowl of high protein dog food. Meg and Scooter are best of pals. He gets no dog treats, and she gets no Blue Bell ice cream. They are inseparable, a rare pair, often seen in the warm rays of the sun taking a nap together. No arguments had yet been settled between the high-jacked dog and the one found by the highway. The outcome of this race would determine who would go to the top of the pecking order in this household. The rules of the race nearly caused a divorce. Mary Ann entered this thing that looked like a long red stretched limousine, manufactured by a dachshund, named Wiggles When She Walks. Wiggles when She Runs would also be a fitting name for her. My entry was the amazing Mattie Grace. The winner of the race would be the top dog, and the owner of the winning dog would be the "He Coon" or the "She Coon" of the household. This race would establish the pecking order if a veto was not employed.

The amazing Mattie Grace won the amazing race, and I soon learned that women are sore losers. I reminded Mary Ann that performance dogs were worth more than show dogs any day and that I would enjoy my position as the "He Coon" in this house. Mattie enjoyed treats before I put her to bed that night, a reward for my exalted position. Boy, was I proud of her.

A promise made must be a promise kept. I bribed Mattie when I told her that if she tightened up and won this race, I would take her to see Tater the next morning. Watching children or dogs at play can be an uplifting experience with enthusiasm and excitement punctuating every moment. The monotony of old age was replaced by the joy of youth in their romps and plays. Mattie was excited to see Tater. Changing his name to King did not change his looks, and he was still long and short. They enjoyed running and playing, jumping and rolling, and chasing the chickens until they were near exhaustion. As I looked at them, I wondered if they remembered their past. "We will come to enjoy another day," I promised.

Children often have imaginary playmates, and adults often have invisible playmates too because they keep them hidden. The honesty of children makes parents cringe at times. Our pastor would call the children down to the front of the church auditorium for children's church each Sunday. Then he asked this question, "Has anything exciting happened at your house this week?" After hearing about several of these exciting things, panicked parents began taking these children home after Sunday school and avoiding church and this question. The pastor noted the drop in attendance at the worship service and solicited the help of the deacon body in fixing the problem. "It's as plain as the nose on your face," I said. "Quit asking that question about anything exciting happening at your house this week." Parents were finally able to take a deep breath during children's church, and attendance returned to normal.

The deep imagination of children makes it hard to tell if imagined playmates or certain stories are real or imagined. Michael was the imagined playmate of my son when he was growing up. Mary Ann sent a lot of cookies, drinks, and treats for Michael to enjoy and listened to a load of blame placed on Michael for things gone wrong and things lost. If the tales about Michael were true, we would have preferred that our son find another friend.

All work and no play can dull our knives and our lives. Free time and play time give the body and mind time to rejuvenate, reinvigorate, revitalize, re-energize, and put the zest back into life. Mattie listened to a lot of stories about the old places I revisited with her and joined me as I explored new ones. One of her favorite pastimes was going to competition rifle matches with me as I participated. Everyone would make her the center of attention and pick on her as if they might harm me. She would always come to defend me as I joined in the fun. Between each target and the next match, I would let her go with me to hang the new target. Competitors placed a sea of forty to more than a hundred wind flags of all shapes, sizes, and colors. This sea of flags was an inviting playground for a rambunctious dog, and Mattie always ran through them like a whirlwind. I told Mattie how much I had enjoyed the friendship and fellowship of my shooting buddies everywhere. I am saddened as I see some of them with painful limps, others with failing eyesight, a few battling cancer and other diseases, reminders that the wear and tear of life is catching up to all of us. The ones who have sent the last round down the range will not be forgotten either, memories that time cannot erase.

As we grow older we often dream that we could live yesterday again. We live so fast we forget to slow down and smell the roses. We need to live as though tomorrow may never come and soak up every minute of each day like a sponge. There are treasures to be found in each moment, keepsakes that cannot be bought or sold. The things I learned about life from Mattie Grace were what "Higher" education is all about. There is a part inside us that never grows old, and I am convinced that a part of a little boy lives in the heart of every old man. I lived yesterday again, as I taught her today, what I learned then.

She learned that she should watch out for snakes, that it was all right to play with frogs and chase butterflies, and that she should not put her paws on a bee. I told her several truths: that there is not a pot of gold at the end of a rainbow; that little girls don't get curly hair if they eat all their spinach; that drinking coffee won't make us black; that life is like the Dow Jones, up one day and down the next; that heaven is only a heartbeat away, and the other place is too. I told Mattie Grace, "I have learned some valuable lessons on my journey of life. Live each day so that you don't have to say I'm sorry. Don't wait until tomorrow to do what you need to do today. If you have any regrets, adopt a puppy."

Our first walk in the woods reminded me of my first visit to this familiar place. The expression on her face probably mirrored the expression on my face on my first visit to this place. The sights, the sounds, and the smells were much keener to her than to an old man whose senses had been dulled and dimmed by time. It was on this walk that she saw her first lizard, smelled her first squirrel, and heard her first owl. I sat on a log and watched her romp and play and roll in the leaves, and I thought that it does not get any better than this. The secret to staying young is inspired by being with the young. I planned our next trip and would pack a lunch.

Throughout my life, the Tensas swamp with the winding river from its inception at Lake Providence to its confluence with the Ouachita River near Jonesville, Louisiana, has been the scene for many excursions. It was here that I killed my first squirrel, saw my first bear, built my first fire, killed my first turkey gobbler and buck deer, roasted a rabbit on an open fire, and wished I could be everywhere at once. Every man should be able to take a boy here for the same reasons. I would put on an old pair of boots I wore out here long ago, pack a delicious lunch, and take Mattie down memory lane. This trip made an old man cry. What was will never be again! "Mattie, I am so sorry for you to see me cry, but coming here always takes me back in time." This place was called the Sportsman's Paradise teeming with all kinds of game, especially deer. Just across the lake on moonlit nights, wolves could be heard howling. A nesting pair of ivory-billed woodpeckers raised their young by the McDonald water hole. A long tailed cat that screamed the night I hunted in McGill bend left tracks that were the same size as military tires on a CJ3A Willis Jeep. A pair of bald eagles caught fish in Upper Fool River and raised their young in a stick nest high in a cypress tree on Eagle Nest Bayou. But something went wrong.... The talk was that global warming came visiting, that the carbon footprint was seen in the area, that DDT and chlorinated hydrocarbons ravaged the nest, and a thousand more reasons hatched to make Bubba and his offspring look ignorant.

Mattie and I walked the old woods road to Lower Lake, now Chain Lake on the map, where we saw a really big alligator and a blue heron fishing near the bank. Two wood ducks startled her when they flew up at Gator Lake when she went to drink water. We walked south down Leading Bayou nearly a half-mile, then east to the McDonald Water Hole. The stump of the tree where the ivory-billed woodpeckers nested had completely rotted and was gone since my last trip here. "Mattie," I said, "sometimes time has a way of erasing memories." The trip back to the house was filled with panic and adventure. We crossed Leading Bayou at the forks in the bayou just north of Francis Lake. The old east and west dummy line was in sight of the horse crossing on the bayou. The steam locomotives used this track line to haul the timber from these woods to the sawmill in Tallulah, Louisiana.

I told Mattie that I shot squirrels in the last of the virgin timber on a ridge close to Pickett Briars. Mattie lapped a little water, enough to quench her thirst, at the spring near the lake and came to sit with me on the old cypress log. The blessing of the food and the blessing of being here were lifted up before we shared the two cans of Vienna sausage. She crawled up into my lap and curled up to take a nap. As I watched her, I wondered what the poor folks were doing. We walked west to where the big white S's were painted on the gum tree—north, south, east, and west on each compass heading. This witness tree marked the intersection of the Township, Range, and Section lines. The tree still stands today, but the long since faded paint serves as a reminder that time marches on.

This walk had been much longer than I had anticipated, and I began to wonder how much more fuel I had left in my tank. Mattie looked like a water bug skitting on top of the water, running here and there. There was no evidence of a tired bone in her body. I was admiring her spunk and energy and thinking back to a day when I could do the same. Suddenly twenty yards up the trail Mattie was four feet in the air, reminding me of someone who pushed a button on a Jack-in-the-Box, and I thought I heard a four-letter word come from her mouth. I knew from past experience that the word I heard was spoken out of a moment of terror. I almost said one myself in the same circumstance. A big timber rattler was coiled and sunning in a blanket of leaves, nearly invisible, when Mattie disturbed him. He surely disturbed her. How to resolve this conflict put me under a tremendous amount of duress.

The philosophy of the balance of nature bunch, the ecological gurus, who moved here in the middle 1980s began to tell Bubba and his descendants that it is wrong to kill snakes. Snakes have as much right to be here as anything else, they say. As I stood to think about this, no one would believe what happened. The ground literally opened up and swallowed that snake up in a huge crack, and the rattling ended. "See, Mattie, I said that no one would believe it, and I wouldn't either if I had not seen it with my own eyes. The memory of this day will always be etched in my heart."

The next trip to the woods and river was where I told her about some simple things. "Mattie, beware of following folks who carry two compasses. They may get you lost if they trust both compasses. The moss always grows on the north side of the tree. A palmetto will make a good fan if you get too hot. A stick will float downstream if the wind doesn't blow too hard. Dry tender can be found in a hollow stump or hole in a tree to start a fire. Mattie, use all of your senses to solve a problem." I would soon give her a test to see if she had been taking notes.

She went around the curve in the woods road about one hundred yards away, and I ran in the opposite direction then off the road to see what would happen. Shortly she came by my position as if she had been shot out of a gun, stopping to see if she could hear me. Then like a bullet she came back by me and out of sight again around the curve. A pitiful begging howl came from her mouth as she looked for sight or sound of me. She must have remembered what I said when I told her, "Use all of your senses to solve a problem."

When she came in sight, she was at a much slower pace with her nose to the ground. She went by where I stepped out of the road and went a short distance before my scent vanished. Immediately she returned to my exit off the road, found my scent, and followed it to find me hiding behind a big tree. I wished people could have looked through those big brown eyes. They would have seen a proud teacher. She had passed the test.

Mattie Grace's passion was treeing squirrels. I first introduced her to squirrels on the back street of the Franklin Parish Courthouse. This site is where bear hunters camped on the bank of Turkey Creek many years ago. I cannot count the times I let her run the squirrels up the trees at this place. People who witnessed her treeing the squirrels would want to buy her. These were the same people who used to refer to her as that mangy mutt. She was my treasure and not for sale. When I would say, "Today is a pretty day to run and play," she would stand on the truck seat looking for squirrels. She would tree more than twenty on a good day, barking up the tree and following them in the timber if they ran. We never killed any, but we had great satisfaction in the chase and the exercise.

When I got home from work, every pretty day was a play day for Mattie Grace, Wiggles When She Walks, and this old man. Energy and calorie burning runs around the house, under the cars, back around the house, under the four-horse trailer, by the brick piles, and under the barn ended in panting exhaustion. After a bit of rest when the instant replay button was pushed, a repeat occurred; or a rewind saw it in reverse. The old man was tired from going both ways. Wiggles had the heart, but not the tools, to compete with Mattie in a foot race. Wiggles was semi-fast, but Mattie was sudden. I was still the He Coon because of her prowess in running, and I was her biggest and best cheerleader. These two were the best of pals romping and playing, a ritual that took place an hour before bedtime each night. I entered the fray every night as the Boogieman to see what kind of watchdogs they would be if I were not at home. The result of a test given to check their senses resulted in this report: hearing is excellent, score A+; vision is excellent, mark A+; smell is sensitive, check OK; taste is not sensitive, likes cat, dog, fish, gerbil, and human foods; touch is suspect, thinks all things are hot or will harm them.

One night, when unannounced, I slowly climbed the stairs to the great room. I barely bumped the wall. Our dogs sounded like a pack of hounds and cur dogs baying hogs in the nearest thicket. Their keen hearing alerted them that strangers might be in the house. Had there been a stranger, he would have assumed that the sound of these voices were of the catch dog variety, pit bulls or airedales or another vicious breed. The barking would lead one to think these two weighed a hundred pounds apiece. Once I heard the madam say, "Marion, is that you?" As I climbed the stairs, the barking became more fierce. Then, "MARION, is that you? If you don't say something, then I am fixin' to shoot through the door." I began to putt, purr, cluck, and yelp like a hen turkey and even threw in a couple of gobbles. These were sounds she had heard from me many times. Since winning the Louisiana State Turkey Calling Contest, I have judged many contests across the country and put on demonstrations of calling. I use my natural voice without benefit of any other type call. I am always asked how I learned this technique. Mary Ann tells the questioner that if they really want to learn these types of calls, all they have to do is roost on the bedpost as I did, and in a week to ten days it will just come natural.

Every night before going to bed I put a size 3XL dark blue flannel shirt over my head and arms, and, out of the dark of the bathroom, I approached the bed. Mattie defended this place with her life, and the show dog dived under the cover and did not make a sound, willing to be a coward to live another day. Mattie bounced all over the bed and solicited Mary Ann's help to stop this monster. This ritual of play was an every night game that both of us enjoyed, and it ended with her laying her head in the bend of my arm, belly up. I would rub her tummy, and shortly after the lights were turned out, she would begin to snore like a little bear in hibernation.

Guineas do not play fair. Mattie saw a guinea preening its feathers between the sand pile and a big stack of bricks. Lesson number one about guineas happened as I pointed at this bird and said, "Sic him." The racket this startled creature made alerted his buddies, who came from every direction to help him. Sixty-three guineas and one dog being too great of odds to suit Mattie, she turned on the after-burners to pass by the brick pile on the way to get my help. As she came by the pile of bricks, a guinea mounted her and wrapped its wings around her neck. This scene looked like a monkey on a football as she headed to the house. A table saw that had been discarded in the back yard got this monkey off her back. Mattie ran through the framing on the saw, and guinea feathers flew everywhere. One addled guinea lay flopping on the ground trying to regain its senses. The decibels of the noise made by all these guineas were nearly deafening. Mattie always made sure that I was on her team and led the charge when chasing guineas.

Many people get into a rut in life, a routine of the usual instead of the unusual, the boring instead of the exciting. All work and no play leads one to become dull rather than remain sharp. There are times in all of our lives when we need a good whetting to sharpen our senses to the things that are most important. There may be a revival of common sense, a spiritual reconnection, or the weighing of true values that will bring renewal and freshness to an otherwise stale life. We should stop long enough to look at a beautiful sunset, listen to the melodies as the birds sing, watch a doe skip along with her fawn, observe a mother hen coaching and coaxing her brood, walk an unfamiliar path, and take along a child, either ours or someone else's. These things more valuable than a facelift are often the source of a soul lift. We must refill our tanks, recharge our batteries, and stop to call an old friend.

An old man and a young dog and the difference in age cause us to think about alternatives. I am on my way to buy an extended mileage package. After I got Mattie, I realized that I needed more miles and more regular tune-ups if we continued to run and play.

Chapter 11

WAGONS WEST

Since I had just bought an extended mileage package, I thought I would take advantage of it on a trip to the Colorado Rockies. I asked Mattie if she remembered my promise when she came to live with us that we would have fun. I said to her, "Sharpen your knife; we are going to the mountains." The local trips to the woods and the Tensas swamps gave me confidence that she was up to this new adventure. I told Mattie, "This old man may need a tune-up, or at least a refill of the prescriptions for the Hadacol and vitamins. Hadacol was a non-prescription vitamin tonic concocted by a candidate for Governor of Louisiana, Dudley J. LeBlanc, in the late 1940s." A young dog whose motor was always running and whose tank was always full would fair just fine on a trek to the mountains.

"Wow, Mattie, you will see sights on this trip that will take your breath away. The beauty of the place may make you think that you are on the outskirts of Heaven." On my first trip there I imagined what it must have been like for the first mountain men who explored this vast wilderness. It was a place of untouched intrusion, a virgin in its innocence. I envisioned myself as a member of the Lewis and Clark Expedition sent on an assignment that would open the door to a new frontier. They used a quill to make a journal entry each day to chronicle this historical event. "Mattie, this is good stuff, and I can hardly wait to tell you the stories around a campfire."

The Rocky Mountains resurrect the pioneering spirit in me each time I go there. Going there is as if I have taken a journey back in time to a primitive place where history was carved for our keeping. This history would die in the ashes of the campfires if it were not for the storytellers of each generation. "Mattie, we will build a ring of rock, we will build a fire with oak and aspen wood, we will smell the smoke mingled with the mountain air, and I will paint a portrait in words so that you can hear the stories like others who have joined me on these trips before." Even though others who beat us there blazed many of the mountain trails, we can live vicariously in their adventures. What stories there are to tell!

I said to Mattie, "We will pack our bags, fill our tanks, charge our batteries, pick our path, and tell folks if they want to hear these stories they better load their wagons if they are going with us."

Time flew by, and the time of our leaving was just around the corner. We planned to have the camp pitched and a pot of coffee on the fire in the rock ring on the night of the harvest moon. This full moon was to occur on September 23rd, the autumnal equinox. A night of such splendor would welcome Mattie to the mountains, and this moment would forever be etched in her memory.

As we left home before the light of day, a gorgeous moon was suspended between the heavens and the earth. Reaching the U.S. Interstate 20 at Delhi, Louisiana, we turned westward looking for the front range of the Rocky Mountains. The moon looked as if it were just loping along over the Interstate Highway, and I told Mattie we would see if we could catch it. When we went over the Red River on the bridge between Bossier City, Louisiana, and Shreveport, Louisiana, the moon disappeared into the roadway just in front of us. I told Mattie that chasing the moon was like her chasing her tail—"sudden" was not quite fast enough to catch it.

Shortly, we crossed over into Texas and saw a sign that read "Welcome to Texas" located at the visitor center at Waskom, Texas. Then no farther than I could throw a rock, things seemed to turn sour. We saw a sign that read, "Don't mess with Texas." I told Mattie, "Get your knife out because these Texans are mad about something, but they better not mess with us." It made no sense to me that a welcome sign was out and now it seemed as if they were trying to pick a fight.

I might as well get it off my chest and confess that I would like to mess with Texas. Somebody said the Creator was near the end of creation when he made Texas. It was rumored that He took all the leftover parts and just threw them down—thus He made Texas. I tease my Texas friends that He made Texas the laughing stock of the world by taking some of these leftover parts and putting horns on frogs and donkey ears on rabbits. One of the institutions of higher learning has a horned frog as a mascot, and some other teams have jackrabbits for theirs. I would like to rearrange some of the creation, and this is what I would do. I would take Texas and make it an island in the middle of the Gulf of Mexico; then, I would sew the hole up left in the map. The trip to the mountains would be so much more pleasant if we did not have to mess with or go through Texas. A person could go anywhere in the world in a day if he did not have to go across Texas. If there were a vote, I would vote to move Texas.

We passed Longview, Texas, crossed the Sabine River, and then passed the sign that advertises the Kilgore and East Texas Oil Museum. "Mattie, one day we may come back to visit, but not this trip. We are going to the mountains to have fun." Thoughts about my hard work when I was in the oil patch puts blisters on my hands and makes my back hurt. The stories about the roughnecks and roustabouts are stones we will leave unturned for another day.

Fast forward with the pedal down to the "Big D," that is, Dallas, Texas. This place looked as if it were a mass of metal ants rushing in all directions. The madness of all this activity is probably fueled by the need to keep up with the Joneses. I told Mattie that I am glad that I am not a part of this rat race. "Look at 'em, Mattie, you will never see this many people in one place ever again. If we had been thinking ahead, we could have brought a truckload of our roosters to sell to finance our trip. Mattie, we could have picked a prime intersection, painted a persuasive sign, propositioned a Dallas Cowgirl Cheerleader to point at the sign that read 'Live Alarm Clocks, Get Yours Now', and pedaled our product to these proud Texans. It is about time for a country boy to slick these city boys out of some of their money."

This bumper-to-bumper traffic, pull-up and stop, pull-up and stop again can burn a clutch out, and cause me to need a patience tune-up. "Mattie, I'm looking for some open road where I can mash on the gas." We left Wichita Falls and Vernon at our backs, and we were looking for Childress. Mattie had been napping on this boring stretch of U.S. Highway 287 since we arrived to intersect it at Decatur.

"Break time," I yelled as I pulled down a county road and parked next to the railroad tracks. We would stretch our legs, eat a snack and treats, and wet our whistles. Then I said, "Mattie, it is all right with me if you mess on Texas, if you are a mind too." And we did! While we were resting and Mattie was exploring Texas, I heard a train whistle and saw the bright light as it descended the distant hill. By several loud blasts of its horn, the big engine sounded its approach to the county road intersection. Mattie Grace saw and heard her first train, but she did not want me to add her name to the passenger list. She would ride with me.

As we passed through Quanah, Texas, I stepped a bit back in time and told Mattie how this town was named. Quanah Parker was a Comanche Indian Chief who led his people against the white settlers. The encroachment of the white man was an ugly stigma on the tribe's way of life. The slaughter of millions of bison forever altered the life of the American Indians. Bison, not buffalo, is the proper name for the North American animal that at one time was estimated to number over sixty million. "Buffalo" and "buffalo hunter" are misnomers when referring to this particular animal. However, both terms may be used in telling this story. "Bison" is the proper name, not "buffalo". Quanah Parker was the son of the Comanche Indian Chief Nokoni and Cynthia Ann Parker, a white captive. Quanah Parker's conflict with the white settlers ended when he surrendered to the United States Army in 1875. In June 1875, this band of Indians was moved to a reservation near Fort Sill in Southwest Oklahoma. The plight of all of the American Indians—Comanche, Apache, Shoshone, Nez Perce, Kiowa, Cherokee, and others—was centered on the slaughter of the animal that was strategic to the Indians' way of life. The Great Father gave this sacred trust to the Indian. The greed of the white man and the building of the railroads to develop the Western United States pushed the bison to near extinction and destroyed the Indians' way of life.

Nearing Childress, Texas, I told Mattie to "Look for 'em," and she saw locomotives on both ends of a very long line of freight cars loaded with coal. A common sight on this stretch of U.S. Highway 287 is coal as it makes its way from the mines to coal powered plants generating electricity for much of our country. We saw another train with over 100 cars loaded with coal before we got to Amarillo. On the trip from Amarillo through the Texas Panhandle, we saw many pheasants as we passed through the towns of Dumas and Dalhart, and we arrived at Clayton, New Mexico. I told Mattie about the National Rifle Association facilities and gun ranges at Raton, New Mexico, and promised a visit there on our next trip. Crossing Raton Pass, we dropped into Trinidad, Colorado, and on to Walsenburg. We could see the twin Spanish Peaks south of La Veta pass. I showed Mattie the Sangre De Cristo mountain range, the front door to the Rockies. I told her that the Supreme Court may change the name one day because it means "The Blood of Christ," and that is offensive to so many. "These are the hills from which our help comes."

The Rocky Mountains are full of phenomenal marvels, and the keys to unlock many mysteries of our past lie here. The mountain ranges tell the stories of the earth's existence before life existed, the pre-Cambrian era, to the very latest of recorded history. The story written in rock is found in igneous, sedimentary, and metamorphic outcroppings; a rich tour through the geological ages is always inviting to a new visitor.

"Mattie, how would you like me to train you to hunt dinosaurs? We will talk about that later. Mattie, men could spend a lifetime here, and it is as if it is just a glance back in time. Mattie, these stories about the mountains have been told around many campfires. Forces from below the crust of the earth caused molten material called magma to form igneous rock. Some are extrusive like basalt and make their way through cracks and fissures to the surface of the earth. Others are intrusive like granite and cool close to the surface. The texture of the rock depends on the rate of cooling. Obsidian cools so rapidly it has the texture of glass and has been used in surgical instruments for cutting. Pumice, on the other hand, cools much slower; and, as the gas bubbles escape, voids are left and the rock is lighter in weight than it appears.

"Sedimentary rock is deposited as a result of weathering, wind, water, and ice. The stratification of these deposits is evidenced by layers of different materials. Shale, limestone, sandstone, boulders, sand, gravel, and coal are examples of these deposits. Rocks and minerals of all kinds can be identified here. The metamorphic rock is a combination of igneous and sedimentary rock that has undergone heat, pressure, or both to change the parent rock. Recrystallization and cleavage are characteristics common to this type rock."

We found sights, scenes, and signs everywhere. Fifty-five peaks over 14,000 feet are in Colorado. The mountains have an abundance of animals: Rocky Mountain goats, bighorn sheep, bear, deer, hares, elk, mink, mountain lions, porcupines, squirrels, chipmunks, coyotes, moose, muskrats, beaver, badger, and other species.

Mattie stood on the highest suspension bridge in the world at the Royal Gorge, 1,053 feet above the Arkansas River. A railroad passes through this canyon that is only thirty feet wide at places. Since Mattie and I were short on funds, we did not rent a parachute to jump off the bridge.

We stopped at a little rock shop down the road, and I showed Mattie a lot of specimens: talc, gypsum, calcite, fluorite, apatite, feldspar, quartz, topaz, corundum, and diamond. I told her, "Mattie, any rock hound would recognize these as the ten rocks on Mohs hardness scale." While showing her other rocks and minerals, I found a large piece of pyrite—then I had a brainstorm—boy, did I have a brainstorm! I bought that rock. "Mattie, when we get home, we will show this to Mary Ann and tell her that we have laid claim to a gold mine. This rock will be our ticket to many more trips out here. Tell me we ain't rich if she buys this story about 'fool's gold.' She may want to invest in this venture herself. Remember, we have to keep a straight face when we tell her."

Mattie was still asleep as we travelled the winding road through the mountain passes past Gunnison, Colorado, to the Blue Mesa Reservoir. As I turned into a lookout I said, "Look for 'em" and interrupted her nap. The expression on her face was my payday—it was worth the whole trip. She had come a long way from the trash pile on the Bayou Macon River in Louisiana to the beautiful Blue Mesa Reservoir on the Gunnison River in Colorado. Not many dogs are privileged to drink from waters so far apart.

The view was both beautiful and breathtaking, and I told Mattie to look for the sign that would tell us how far heaven was. Continuing on, we traveled to Montrose, then Delta, then again across the Gunnison River to Orchard City where I always stop. The apple orchards here have served a lot of Granny Smith apples for apple tarts cooked in Dutch ovens on my campfires. I told Mattie that I call this angel food, and we would eat our fill since we were angels.

I pointed out the irrigation practices in raising onions, potatoes, corn, vegetables, alfalfa, and other crops. I explained the issues of water rights, and the importance to this region. We turned at the old stone church in Eckert, passed through the apple orchards, down hill past the landfill, and to the sheep ranch. The pens were full of lambs and ewes; these were animals Mattie had never seen.

Cedaredge, the little town nestled among the apple orchards in the valley, marks a climb up a winding road to the top of the Grand Mesa. It was as if an artist hung a canvas and began to paint a picture to capture what our eyes were seeing. Mattie's big brown eyes looked in all directions as she stood in my lap. I wished I could know her thoughts. Was she looking at the picture, or was she looking for the Painter?

We turned off Highway 65 onto Lands End Road and Flowing Park Road to find the Bull and Brown Trail near Flowing Park Reservoir. We chose a spot and quickly pitched the tent. This place was to be our home away from home, our first night in camp.

A promise made is a promise to keep. We built the ring of rock; we gathered the wood for the fire; we brewed a fresh pot of coffee, and the mountain air mingled with the smoke and began to stir the memories of days in the past. "Mattie Grace, tonight you will see the magnificent miracle of the Master and why I am drawn to these mountains like a magnet. The memories of my visits over the last forty-five years are much clearer than my first ones over sixty years ago. Mattie, the beauty of this place and the nights bathed in splendor will forever be etched in my memory. The harvest moon, the magic of the moment, and the measure of many men and their stories will make you hungry for more of this place."

There are many stories buried in the ashes of the campfires I built in the rock rings over the years. I have sat with men whose heartaches left scars in their hearts and with others hurt by the hand that life dealt them. Some shared that they had been pursuing dreams and chasing rainbows and spent their lives building on the sand, rather than on the rock. I am confident that these confessions are as safe as the ashes scattered by the wind because they will never be pieced together again for other ears to hear. A promise made must be a promise kept.

Men have left here different than they came, as if there were healing in the smoke. They were better and stronger, changed and challenged. "Mattie, do you remember when I told you that whittling on a stick and cutting too many hay strings would dull your knife? I was really talking about the wear and tear of life that can dull our lives. It is as important to sharpen our lives as it is to sharpen our knives."

Sitting around the campfire, I told Mattie when I was a young boy that I heard a lot of stories and tales about hunting trips and camping experiences. Successful hunters display buckhorns and bear skins, turkey beards and coon hides, rattlesnake rattlers and hornet nests, and other trophies on their walls. I was chomping at the bit, waiting for my chance to enter this fraternity. One can become so reckless and careless that he can become deaf, dumb, and blind.

The McManus boys, Hollis and Shelby, were experienced and were reputed to be good at this game. They decided to lead and teach me. They expressed that snipe hunting was not for the faint-hearted and that this trial was to see if I could be depended on for a hunt after bigger game.

"Mattie, I should have smelled a rat." The shadows of darkness were swallowing up the leftovers of the daylight as we drove down a lonely stretch of gravel road and turned onto a bumpy turn-row. A sea of grass was soon to be the scene of a world-class snipe hunt.

I swallowed this story hook, line, and sinker. I should have known something was up since I had never seen a snipe displayed on any hunter's wall.

Each night at the supper table, Hollis and Shelby talked about the dangers lurking everywhere in the forest. Each night they talked about seeing panthers on their hunts, hearing them screaming at night, and finding carcasses left from their kills. I was told that bears, wolves, wildcats, and poisonous snakes might be encountered on these hunts as well.

On the night we went snipe hunting, we unloaded the tools of our trade from the back of an old plank-sided Chevy truck. The inventory included a forked stick about fifteen inches long, a small piece of rope about eighteen inches long, and a burlap or grass type sack. Not wanting to raise any eyebrows, I did not know if they said "toad-sack" or "tote-sack," but I chose not to show my ignorance by asking. We were going to fill it up with snipe no matter what it was called.

"Mattie, I think I know how you felt when you were left at the thicket." My guides walked me to a shallow V ditch, propped the sack open with the stick, and told me to tie the sack up with the rope when it was full of snipe. "Did I understand?" they asked before leaving. Understand—not then, but soon I would. There was no drive, they did not do the hard part, they set me up, they laughed at me, and they downright lied.

It got quiet ... I mean really quiet and really dark. Then I felt something creep up from about my belt line to the middle of my back. I learned later that it was a yellow streak and that I was not as brave as I thought I was. I still hold the unofficial world record for running the mile to the house. Bubba, the southern redneck, never went snipe hunting. They said he was too smart to fall for that trick.

Without saying a word, I walked in the direction of the Flowing Park Reservoir. Mattie skipped along and played with her shadow that was cast by the gorgeous harvest moon. This half-mile walk and back again would let us shake the kinks out of our legs from the long trip here. As the moon splashed its beauty upon the waters of the reservoir, we soaked up reflections that would be remembered for the rest of our lives. As we stood on the big flat rock at the water's edge, Mattie stood to put her paws on my legs. I knew this little tyke wanted me to pick her up. As I sat on the rock, I picked her up to hold her in my arms; and her "thank yous" did not come in a Hallmark card, but rather from her heart. "Mattie," I said, "the beauty of this place makes me think that heaven must not be very far away." She lapped water from the reservoir until her tank was full.

The past thirty hours without any sleep about emptied my tank and drained my battery. A breath of crisp mountain air kissed the back of my neck as I closed the flap on the tent and blew out the lantern. Then the pooch I rescued from the pile of junk joined me as the sleeping bag swallowed us up for a night of sleep. I whispered, "Mattie Grace, I love you so much. Thank you for coming with me."

The moon accented the blanket of frost as ice crystals glistened on the blades of grass. This sight was a beautiful welcome mat for our first morning. Stirring in the ashes and embers, I stoked the fire into a roaring inferno, and the old cowboy coffee pot served up another cup, freshly brewed. While it was simmering, Mattie and I walked to stand on the rim rock on top of the Grand Mesa. It was as if a giant hand began to roll up a curtain as we faced to the east and the light of another day approached. Just down the hill from where we stood, a carpet of fog reached all the way to the towering mountain peaks of the Continental Divide in the distant east. A huge ball of fire slowly climbed over the horizon, and the sight made a little dog's tail wag the whole dog. Mattie's sharp bark to announce a new day was her way of wishing that Little Man could see this sight.

After the morning breakfast I told Mattie we needed to get some supplies and see some local sights. The thick fog slowed our descent into the valley below and obscured our view of things I wanted to show Mattie. Two monadnocks were standing in the valley looking as if they were sentries or soldiers guarding the landscape. These granite columns were left exposed when glaciers eroded softer material from around them. These two stood as testimonies to time . . . the old in the midst of the new and the hard left exposed by the soft. These stories changed with time.

The morning sun ran the fog out of the valley, and evidence of a changing of seasons arrested our attention. Accenting the landscape, green alfalfa fields were scattered here and there in the apple orchards where branches were burdened with ripening fruit. The green of the cedar in the midst of the reds and browns of the oak brush was a prelude to a spectacular view farther up the hill. The sun of the morning made the aspen appear to be on fire. Beautiful colors of green, yellow, scarlet, purple, and red blended together looking as if flames were leaping through the timber. A backdrop of pine and Douglas fir gave strength to a viewer's heart. We were a part of this picture as we returned to camp.

Soon after the apple tarts were fried in the cast iron skillet, three Texans drove up to the camp. With introductions and handshakes, Sammy, Bubba, and Tommy met Mattie and me. A cup of coffee from the old cowboy coffee pot and an apple tart are always better than a handshake in making friends. "Why are you here?" they asked. I told them "The Matter of Grace Story," about Mattie and me, and the day I picked her up out of a trash pile. Mattie's story seemed to warm their hearts as they smelled the angel food in the smoke. Mattie and I rolled the welcome mat out and welcomed these Texans to our food and our fire. The cast iron cookware was always the featured attraction in the ring of rock. Tonight it would serve up a cowboy stew, southern cornbread, Louisiana rice, fresh apple tarts, and freshly brewed coffee. Watching this hungry bunch eat reminded me of feeding the dogs or slopping the hogs.

After supper I began to tell the night's stories by saying that the United States hit a home run when it acquired the Louisiana Purchase from France. Thomas Jefferson made the treaty on April 30, 1803, during his first administration as President of the United States of America. The treaty was signed on May 2, 1803, and it reached Washington on July 14, 1803. The land from the Rocky Mountains to the Mississippi River and from the Canadian border to the Gulf of Mexico was purchased for 15 million dollars. The

827,987 square miles added part or all of 15 states to the continental United States.

Thomas Jefferson appointed Meriwether Lewis, a U.S. Army Officer, to lead an expedition to explore the new acquisition from France and to look for a passage to the Pacific Northwest. Lewis enlisted the help of William Clark, another Army Officer, to lead this exploration jointly as a team. Meriwether Lewis was a naturalist who had an interest in collecting plant, animal, rock and mineral specimens from the trip. William Clark was a keeper of records who charted the journey on maps and later published the journals of the trip.

The group departed from a camp near St. Louis, Missouri, in May 1804. They traveled up the Missouri River and wintered in North Dakota. The French Canadian trader and interpreter, Toussaint Charbonneau, along with his young Shoshone Indian wife, Sacajawea, joined the party there. Sacajawea was immortalized by stories told about her. She served as an interpreter, acquired horses from her brother who was an Indian Chief, and gave birth to a child while on the expedition.

The party crossed the Rocky Mountains in late summer and followed the Clearwater, Snake, and Columbia Rivers to arrive at the Pacific Ocean in November 1805. They spent the winter in Oregon and began the trip home in March 1806. Except for a few deviations, the group returned following nearly the same route and arrived back in St. Louis in September 1806. Thomas Jefferson appointed Meriwether Lewis as the Governor of the Louisiana Territory in 1807. People think he committed suicide in 1809; however, it may have been a murder.

We all agreed this was a great transaction that benefited our country. We hope that our current leaders do not squander it with reckless decisions. Our concern is that spiraling spending may sap all the collateral from our resources. The cry for more, if heeded, will finally kill us.

Stories, stories, and more stories emerged before the curtain fell on this night. The story about Mattie brought a barrage of questions from the Texans. They knew by now that she was my ears, that she was my eyes, and that she was a treasure to my heart. Tomorrow the trails would test an old man, and a young dog would test the trails. It remained to be seen whether the Texans could keep up. I whispered to Mattie, "We will test them Texans tomorrow to see if they are mountain tough."

The hikes on the next three days took us to the Battlement reservoirs, down Dirty George Creek to Granby Ditch, up the Blue Grouse Trail to Point Camp Trail, and back to camp on the Bull and Brown Trail. The script of this trip on the trails was showcased in the sights and sounds and will be told in stories on another trip. These scenes seem to have a sacred signature that makes one think they are in a secluded sanctuary. "Mattie, I just know it. Heaven is not very far from here." Sights and sounds and stories filled the days with fun and fellowship, and new friendships were forged that would last a lifetime.

As she treed squirrels everywhere along the trail, Mattie provided a morning matinee that was a masterpiece. I told those Texans there was not enough oil in Texas to buy Mattie. I bragged and said I would bet she would have been good at hunting dinosaurs if we had lived back then. Mattie's interest quickly changed; something had arrested her attention; she wanted me to hear what she heard; she wanted me to know what she knew; and she wanted me to sense what she sensed. Nobody had a clue, but Mattie—three Texans and an old man with eyes glued to a motionless little dog. Then just under the break of the hill, something knocked a rock loose to roll down the mountain. "What was it?" I thought. "Was it a mountain lion, deer, human, or bear?" Then a scream sent Mattie scrambling to stand next to me. Willie, the mule, would have thought it was a lion too. I had got out more than my knife, and the three Texans were standing close to an old man that always keeps his gun cocked.

A big bull elk bugled boldly as he followed his harem onto the trail in front of us. I yelled sic 'em as loud as I could. Barking every step of the way, a seven-pound brave little dog disappeared into the dust after a 700-pound bull elk. That stampede won the hearts of those Texans toward Mattie as her worth increased in their eyes.

I showed Sammy, Bubba, and Tommy the old rail fence that the old-timers used to trap wild horses. Now a casualty of time, the fence, much like me, was in a lot better shape forty-five years ago. We saw several grouse along the trail and remarked about the delicious meal they would make for hungry men. I pointed out the practice of making water ditches years ago by plowing them on contours along the mountainsides descending gradually to bring drinking water to the towns below. Boy, have times changed! The water gates that fed the pipeline next to Dirty George Creek are no longer maintained; they have been abandoned.

The descent downhill with the daypack reminded us it was filled with a mountain meal, a real deal. We welcomed the drinks and dessert. This rough rocky road began a descent from the Blue Grouse Trail to the Porter Reservoir Road. "Look for the crookedest aspen tree you have ever seen as a rock table awaits us there," I said. All three Texans pointed at the same time and said, "That's it." "Mattie Grace, give thanks," I said. She placed her head on outstretched paws, and paused, and Someone else came to share this spread. Mattie's bark was the "Amen" that ended the silence. These men said that they had never seen a dog pray, and I said, "You ought to see her preach." Mattie stories were the subject of this session at the rock. These stories told about Mattie and me, how we both walked away from our past and met up on our way to the Big House, and how we have been blessed along the way.

Thirteen years ago, we were here on an elk hunt, and J. D. McCoy, a friend from Spearman, Texas, and I saw a bad sight here at the cattle gap. We drove up in a jeep and saw a cow standing next to the road with her calf standing by her side. A sad sight indeed, a starving calf, was unable to nurse because of a muzzle filled with porcupine quills. A curious calf came too close to this cranky critter and nearly ended up as a corpse. The mama cow with a strutted udder needed some relief from her condition. We made plans to get

Willie and a lariat at the campsite just up the road. The spurs convinced Willie that this mad mama was not a lion but rather a belligerent beast that nearly caused a wreck. McCoy stood guard with an oak brush limb to keep the mad cow out of the fray. After roping the calf we pulled eight porcupine quills from its nose and mouth with a pair of pliers. A hungry calf and a happy cow found help from human hands. I told Mattie and the three Texans, "A playful gesture with a porcupine can wreck the day and send you to an early grave."

The camp at the top of the Bull and Brown Trail is all uphill from the cattle gap. The trail was a true test for the Texans, and their temperatures rose with the trail. Mattie and I left them scattered up the hill, casualties of charley horses and cramps, and went to start supper. I told Mattie, "The mountains will toughen the Texans if they don't kill'em first." A sip of Hadacol is better than a Hot Shot (electric cattle prod), when the trail gets steep. Steaks and bakes and stories fed us for another night. Their shouts, moans, and groans caused by their charley horses and cramps interrupted the stories at the campfire. For three days we laughed at the Texans, and we laughed with the Texans. They were as full of life as any bunch I have ever seen. They were as funny as a boatload of monkeys.

This trip was one to remember. An old man, a young dog, and three Texans all said this happening was a God Thing. We made a promise to meet again as we blew out the light and loaded the wagons for the trip back home. A promise made is a promise to keep.

Chapter 12

THE TALE THAT
WAGGED THE DOG

M attie's life was like a tale that is told. She had a complete
metamorphosis from without and from within that would
remind one of the transformation from an ugly worm to a beautiful butterfly. At first if someone had taken Mattie to be auctioned,
nobody else would have bid. She was like an uncut and unpolished
diamond passed over by those who only had eyes for glitz and
glamour. The sparkle in those big brown eyes convinced me that
she would be the perfect gem. Tongues began to wag, telling the tale
that too many mule wrecks, too many brain tumors, too many heat
strokes, and too many gunshots had me shell shocked and brain-
damaged. As evidence, people pointed to a mangy dog that followed
me, and they implied that no one in his right mind would do such
a thing. These people had pity for the dog and talked to the proper
authorities about getting some treatment for me. I pointed out to
them that the dog was the one sick with the mange and they needed
to have pity on me and help me pay for her treatment.

One of the identifying factors in someone's life is his reputation
or certain characteristics that sets him apart. Some people live their
lives in black and white while others are colorful characters that live
their lives in Technicolor. Some folks live bland lives, unflavored
and without taste. Mattie's life was full of pep and vinegar and flavored just right, and she was voted Miss Congeniality because she

had personality plus. The flame of love in Mattie's heart was fanned from the embers and ashes of a nearly ruined life. I first met her as a fearful creature, but she became my faithful companion. A man can tell a dog things he cannot tell his wife or best friend. Few and far between are members of the human tribe that we can trust with the secrets of our hearts. The statement is nearly always true that if two people know of a matter, it is no longer a secret. The most valued qualities of friendship are confidence and trust, qualities that cannot be guaranteed by money or position.

The adventure of life should be like a flower garden, changing each day and allowing the arrangement of a new bouquet every day. The table of life should never be set with leftovers. The menu needs to change so that things do not grow stale. A long-faced sourpuss can steal the joy out of any room as if the sun went behind the clouds. Occasionally there are personalities like Mattie Grace who shine like the sun when they are present.

The stories of Mattie's allegiance emerged in the circles I traveled. She believed she owned me, and I just played her game. The story of the ten lepers in Luke 17:11-19 reminds me of Mattie's life before she was cured of the mange that had cursed her life. The sentence of separation caused the lepers to wander, banned to a lonely existence. Their only hope was in their pleas for mercy from the Master. The story clearly states that ten lepers were healed, but that only one returned to fall at the Master's feet to thank him. No act of gratitude, no gesture of appreciation, no acknowledgement, and no thank you note came from the other nine. The grateful one who returned to thank the Master was a Samaritan. The man that has a heart full of thanksgiving will never have a frown on his face. Mattie's cup was always filled with joy as it was poured out from a thankful heart. People began to talk and tongues began to tell the tale of a dog found beside the road who, like the leper, displayed an attitude of gratitude. They talked about how she rode everywhere with me. "Mattie," I told her, "I'm so glad that you're not afraid of riding with me since tales of my fast driving have circulated for years."

Many years ago I saw a news clip on a national news channel of Pope John Paul's visit to a foreign country. When he exited the airplane, he got down on his knees and kissed the ground. I thought they must have scared him real bad, and that this gesture was an act of thanksgiving that he had arrived safely. I told Mattie that this scene reminded me of a trip I took with a friend of mine forty-eight years ago. "Mattie, my friend wrote an account of this trip and gave it to me recently. Here is the story in his own hand."

Remembering the "Fast Back"

People who've known me over the last 40 years know that I love sixty era "muscle" cars. The story I'm about to tell involves a trip I took in the very first muscle car that I ever encountered. The year was 1963.

Most people my age and older can remember what they were doing when they heard about President Kennedy's death. To set the stage for describing this event, the exact time was a few months before JFK's assassination in 1963. The Vietnam War was just heating up and it was still several years before man went to the moon. I had just finished my freshman year at Louisiana Tech, and was nearing my 19th birthday. Getting back to college for the fall semester depended upon me getting a summer job so I could make enough money to pay my school expenses for the next year. Summer jobs for students had been scarce and it was already mid July. I knew that I had to do something fast.

My good friend, "M.C.," who had been working in the Texas oil fields for several months, called me up one Saturday morning to make good on his promise to help me find summer work. The conversation went something like this:

"Meet me Sunday afternoon at 6:30 p.m. sharp in front of Jeannette's Drive-In," he said in his usual stern voice, "You be there and I'll take you back to Texas with me where a good-paying job will be waiting for you."

I told him I'd be there, on time, and ready to travel. I spent the rest of the day telling my family and friends about my good fortune. In fact, I was so excited that night I hardly slept a wink.

M.C. had just bought the prettiest vehicle I'd ever seen. It was a brand new "1963-1/2" Ford Galaxie 500, a/k/a "Fastback." It was candy apple red, white leather interior, and it was equipped with everything imaginable at the time; including a high performance, 390 cubic inch engine, 4 barrel carburetor, 4-speed transmission, a state of the art AM/FM stereo-phonic radio, and very "rare" air conditioning. Wow, was that car fine! I was very excited about going on a trip in his beautiful new ride, not to mention the job that he had arranged for me.

When it finally came time for us to leave we said our goodbye and were headed out about 6:45. As we pulled out of Jeannette's Drive-In on the north side of town, M.C. told me that our work shift began at midnight and we had to travel about 400 miles in the next five hours or we'd be late for work.

Four hundred miles in five hours? No four-lane highways in those days. Hmmmm, I thought. No problem, M.C. remarked, we'll make it with time to spare. Little did I know that events of the next few hours would be branded in my forehead forever.

Within fifteen minutes of leaving, we were already twenty miles out of Winnsboro, Louisiana, and cruising along at 85 mph or so. That wasn't too bad and it was kinda normal for us country boys to cruise at that speed for short periods of time . . . like maybe 10-15 minutes on our best roads. In my excitement of asking questions about my new job, it seemed like only a couple of minutes before we arrived in Monroe, some 40 miles from home.

In those days our best route to Texas was United States Highway 80, a coast-to-coast highway, but having only two lanes of traffic. Sunday afternoons were often crowded with weekend travelers and 18-wheelers nose to bumper. This day was no exception. By the time we made Shreveport, we must have passed 100 vehicles each time darting in and out of oncoming traffic, all the while not one even came close to passing us. The new Ford Fastback was humming along at 110, or so, miles per hour in the straight-a-ways. While M.C. was enjoying every second of the Daytona 500 driving conditions, this ride was beginning to really frighten the daylights outta me, but what could I say? What could I do? What should I do, I thought? Nothing, except hold on and keep my mouth shut! I really needed that job badly and I wasn't about to screw it up by behaving like a wimp, even though this ride was beginning to seem like being on a run-a-way freight train. I love my job, I love my job, I love my job . . . I kept telling myself in an attempt to take my mind off the howl of that four-barrel carburetor.

M.C.'s self-confidence level was extremely high and he was, after all, a very good driver. Many of us who knew him considered him to also be "bullet proof." He had the right stuff to have been a test pilot, motorcycle daredevil, or a helicopter machine gunner. He wasn't scared of nothing . . . not even dying.

Okay, back to that night. After getting through Shreveport, M.C. told me that we would make better time once we got on the Texas farm-to-market roads. He remarked there was a lot less traffic on them and they were wide, well maintained roads. Just how much faster could we go, I thought? Ford sure had picked an appropriate nickname— "Fastback" for this new car!!!

Once we reached Texarkana, Texas, and got away from U.S. Highway 80 traffic, M.C. really "pinned the ears back" on that red car and began whipping those 390 horses unmercifully. The speed-ometer needle went past 120 and out of sight into the dash. It stayed there for what seemed like an eternity. We must have been going 140 or so at times. It became deathly quiet except for the noise made by the big engine screaming through the night. I gave up on trying to talk so M.C. could devote his undivided attention to driving. By this time, all the money that oil field job was going to pay didn't mean a darn thing to me. After all, I thought, I'd been poor all my life and it really ain't that bad, especially the "being alive" part. By now, all I could think about was daylight coming and buzzards would be pecking out my eyeballs on the side of some Texas hillside. I wondered what inscription would be on my tombstone...maybe, it would be something simple like "Gone but not forgotten." Well, it won't much matter. Oh, Lord just take me quick and painlessly, I kept thinking!

Well, by the grace of God, we made it that night in spite of every-thing. We even got to work on time...with a few minutes to spare, just like ole M.C. had said. I was completely wasted, both physically and mentally. I'll never forget the look on that roughneck's face who saw me kiss the ground as I crawled out of that red car onto the well site parking lot. Not once, over the years, have I ever really let

M.C. know just how scared I was that night. I have no doubt that he sensed it, but he's never let on nor kidded me in any manner. By the way, that was my only trip to ever take with him to this day. In fact, it was probably 30 years afterward before I had the nerve to even get in the same car with him.

On the serious side, my trip to Texas with M.C. represented the beginning of my adulthood and was my very first job away from the Franklin Parish farm. Looking back, that job has meant more to me than mere words can describe. Although I've since changed professions a couple of times over the years, I've never been without a job since that mid-night shift began so long ago. I consider that event as being the crossroads of my life, the beginning of a path that eventually led me to my wonderful wife, and two lovely daughters. I would not have either of the three of them had it not been for the frightful ride. I often wonder what my destiny would have been had I not gotten that particular job opportunity forty some odd years ago.

My good buddy, M.C. left the oil fields and chose another profession himself shortly after he did me this great favor. Since that time he's spent his life helping others, one way or another, just as he helped me. Most of you, from back home in Franklin Parish, Louisiana, will know who M.C. is without me calling his name. He still lives around close by and his long list of righteous acts are widely known. I will always consider his friendship to be one of God's greatest gifts to me, and to the community I still like to call home, as well.

One final note about my friend. Recently he picked up a hitchhiker out in West Texas who rode with him to Rayville, Louisiana. He was a quiet man, didn't have much to say, but as he was getting out, he turned as if to say thanks, but quietly remarked, "Mister, I've been paying attention to your driving, and you know what....there has not been one vehicle pass us since we left El Paso."

Larry Bradley
Crowville High School,
Class of 1962
November 16, 2005

Larry walked into my office forty-two years after this ride and personally thanked me for something I had nearly forgotten. This trip was another down memory lane, a visit back in time to memory lane filled my cup, and I took another drink. It was good to the last drop. Larry then gave me a book of statistics about this 63 ½ XL Ford, the owner's manual, a replica of the car, and the note. Treasures like these that are seasoned with friendship are priceless.

When Mattie Grace came to live in the tin-topped house, happiness moved here. A playful friend arrived, and an old man began to look for the Hadacol left over from yesteryear to give him a shot of energy. The arresting look in Mattie's big brown eyes, ears stuck straight out at half mast, the schnorkie haired face, the salt and pepper curly coat, and a tail that she constantly wagged were the signatures of her life. Mattie's life was a constant expression of love and thanksgiving, a witness of her faithfulness. Her life was a testimony to others and to me of how we ought to treat the One who rescued us. She loved me just as I am. She never told me to pick up my clothes or to take the garbage out or to raise the toilet seat, and she never reminded me that I forgot her anniversary. She would not have changed one thing about me even if she could.

There are some people who feel it is their business to change us and everything else they can. This opinionated bunch will freely offer advice about how to do things, but they will never demonstrate by example how to do it. I remember flying my airplane each night to hold revival services in a small farming town in South Arkansas. After the service the first night, a petite old woman, certainly not a lady, waited until almost everyone had left. She looked me in the eye and said, "Young man, I would not have stood in the pulpit and said what you said tonight." The gentleman in me took it like a man as I nodded my head, smiled, and silently thought, "Yep, and that is why He didn't call you to preach." The next night I flew in early and was dropped off at the church by a local farmer. I sat on the front pew and began to mark a new Bible with a red carmine pencil to highlight certain verses, a practice of mine for years. Being engrossed in this task, I failed to hear anyone until she snatched my Bible from my hands. Again the petite, dried up old woman stood before me, "Young man, what on earth are you doing marking up that Sacred Book?" she said. "Oh, I'm just marking out what I don't like," was my reply. She very near swallowed her teeth. I spent the rest of the week mending fences with this old battleaxe. The last night of the revival this petite, sweet little ole lady handed me a package of homemade tea cakes like my grandmother used to make for my trip home. "Young man, you are the best preacher I ever heard," she said. My cup ran over because of her change of heart, and others also experienced a God Thing.

A life will speak louder than words about a life. Mattie was like my shadow, and she followed me everywhere I went. If I were to leave her in the truck to run into a place of business or make a quick stop somewhere, people wanted to know where Mattie was. It seemed that they had rather see her and have her around more than me. All but one person at the Franklin Parish Sheriff's Office spoiled Mattie with attention by feeding her. The Chief Deputy would stomp and shuffle his feet at her, and she would run behind me for help and protection. He was only picking on her, but this was serious business with her and something she never forgot. She could recognize his presence in the building by sound or smell even though he was not close by. Her growls and grumblings caused him to agitate her just so that she would run to me for protection. This play was just a game with us, but Mattie was thinking about how to pay him back.

The Chief Deputy's office was in the main courthouse building. She would visit him only if she were in my arms. I was her refuge. The deputy would talk rough to her and ask, "What are you doing in my office? You are an ugly mutt. You better get out of here." I always told him that Mattie was a paying customer just like me and that we paid taxes on the goods and services that paid his salary to help run this show. "You'd better be good to her because I may also register her to vote," I threatened.

One time Mattie went with me to the police jury office to take care of some right-of-way business for the water company. As I came back down the hall and through the sheriff's office, I noticed Mattie was not in the hall. Seeing that the Chief Deputy was not in his office, she stopped by to make a deposit directly under his chair, a big pile of number two. I did not know about this incident until later. Since Mattie had never had an accident before, I fully believe that she made this accident on purpose. She wagged her tail proudly and seemed to have a smile on her face when she came out of his office.

Mattie walked with me a long way back in time as I told her about other companions that had previously joined me on this journey of life. I told her about Missy, the solid white pointer with a tint of lemon on the tip of her right ear. Missy's nose and passion for bobwhite quail was unsurpassed. She had a gift to point, back, and retrieve that was unequaled. At the top of her game she was a beautiful picture to watch. I was a college freshman when she put the last bird in my hand. She went to sleep in my arms the night she went to the Big House because time came to claim her. I saw it coming, but there was nothing I could do.

I told Mattie about Dan, a big, fast, and strong liver and white pointer that was headstrong. This trait of Dan could cause a preacher to cuss. I hunted Dan several years before my vocabulary changed. Since I was a sprinter and not a marathon runner, I hunted him from the back of a horse to keep him in sight. After I had a change of vocabulary, I joked that I gave him to a man who could call him what he was. Actually I gave him to my father-in-law when Mary Ann and I left for school at the New Orleans Baptist Theological Seminary. I fed a bunch of people with the quail shot over him.

Tony was a Walker-July hound cross. He was black and tan in color, and he was a deer running machine. I bought Tony from a blind man who hunted fox and coyotes in field trials, but he was a cull that liked the smell of deer better. There was no quit in him. By the time he was three years old, he would run nothing but a buck deer. On a track he sounded like three or four dogs bawling, squealing, chopping, and yodeling, making a heck of a noise. If Tony heard a gunshot or smelled gunpowder ahead on the track, he turned on the afterburner.

Buck and April, the American Saddle Horses, were half brother and half sister. The Tensas swamp was never host to a finer pair of seasoned woods horses that were both gaited and smooth. I would bet every penny I have that these two carried more buck deer from these woods than any other pair. Near the water trough in her thirty-third year, April died of undetermined causes.

Buck lacked twenty days living until his fortieth birthday. I knew that one day his time would come because of his failing health. I could not watch him go through another cold winter because no amount of feed could stop his weight loss. His steps had become too painful for him. When I made up my mind that it was his time, I loved on him in a special way for the next three days and said my goodbyes. I led him out in the pasture next to April's grave. He never heard the shot. I buried them side-by-side, and I will carry memories of them to my grave.

"Mattie, there are others that have added joy to our home—dogs, cats, raccoons, squirrels, skunks, and Fireball." A friend of mine caught Fireball in a corncrib, and he came to live with us about twenty-five years ago. A flying squirrel is an exotic and entertaining bundle of energy like a trapeze artist. Dr. George Gowan did not remember taking the Hippopotamus Oath, the one for taking care of animals, when he ran a man out of his office for bringing a lion for him to worm. When Fireball came for his yearly vaccinations, Dr. Gowan broke out the welding gloves and did the honors. He said a flying squirrel could not eat him, but a lion might.

"Mattie Grace, you have helped keep my memories alive by letting me go back in time. These tales and experiences began when I was a young boy and have spanned a lifetime. I have taken you to places and shared with you stories that helped shape my life and define who I am and what I am. I cannot imagine one man who has been more blessed than me, because life has been so good to me. Mattie, you have heard that bunch say they think I am crazy, but I would like to ask them some questions and let you be the judge of who is crazy." Why do people buy life insurance? The one who pays the premium can only benefit if he dies. The insurance company gambles that he is going to live. Why do we buy house insurance? The homeowner bets that the house will be destroyed, and the insurance company thinks a disaster will never come. Why do people buy burial insurance? It makes no sense to me to bet that I will cheat the undertaker by dying young so that he will be the loser. Benefitting from these insurance decisions makes no more sense to me than trying to win the lottery. "Mattie, before you vote about who is crazy or not, remember the hand that feeds you."

The shadows began to lengthen as we passed by the graves of our family of pets. The setting sun in the west is a reminder of another day that is nearly done. A great big thank you flows out of my heart for having let me walk here. I can clearly see the handwriting on the wall and the stop sign just down the road. I brought Mattie to stand in front of the tin-top house and said, "This is where to bury the rest of me when I move to the Big House."

I told Mattie, "Come on and let's go. I have more stories to tell and places to go. Mattie, slow down, so I can keep up." The adventure continued with this story about a Tale that Wagged the Dog and a dog that wagged her tail.

Chapter 13

STORIES I TOLD MATTIE

No Cats on this Roof

O ne day I said, "Mattie, I want to tell you the story about the tin-topped house and why it is built like this." Then I told her this story. Mary Ann and I lived in a small frame house just across the road from my crop dusting strip. Several family pets also made it their home. Watching Mary Ann trying to round them up at night so that they would be safe inside was funnier than a goat roping. Putting them up at night was a game with them, and they used any tactic to stay on the prowl. The cats climbed light poles and trees and then jumped off onto the top of the house to keep her from catching them. Often this hilarious spectacle of catching them became a battle of wits. With the outcome always in doubt, this practice was dangerous to Mary Ann, and no amount of pleading from me convinced her otherwise. If cats were in trees or on the housetop, she refused to leave them outside. She would get a ladder from the barn and make an assault to catch this wayward bunch. My worry was not for the cats. The dishwasher did not need a broken arm or leg, and the house slave did not need to miss a day's work. Her argument that the animals could not get down by themselves held no water with me. Has anyone ever seen a cat carcass on top of a telephone pole, a pile of bones in a tree, or a decaying body on a rooftop? If animals can get up, they can get down. I told Mary Ann of the consequences of continuing this ridiculous behavior.

The next day was hectic at the flying service with comings and goings, takeoffs and landings, fertilizing wheat, and spraying burn-down on corn ground. I could not believe what I saw as I landed for another load. I saw a ladder propped up on the roof of our carport, a cat disappearing over the hipped roof, and a woman in hot pursuit. Then I remembered the consequences as I ran for the truck and tore out for the house like I was going to a fire. I slid to a stop and jumped out, threw the ladder into the back of the truck, and left as though I were headed to another fire. In the rearview mirror, I saw a woman jumping up and down as if she were on a pogo stick, waving her arms in a crazy fashion. I thought her cuckoo had hung up and driven her crazy.

I drove to the local café where a neighbor of mine was leaving from his morning coffee break. When I asked him if he could do something for me, he said he would if he could. I asked him to stop at my house on his way home to see if he could talk Mary Ann into coming down off the roof. I told him I thought she must have lost her mind in the night because I could not get her down. He turned into our drive as I left with the next load of burndown. Mary Ann was still jumping up and down and waving her arms to attract attention, and she was thankful to see our neighbor. She explained to him that I was not aware that she was on the roof after the cats, I left with the ladder in a hurry, and she was trapped. My return to the airport found him waiting for me. He implied that I had misrepresented the account of what happened since she seemed to be of sound mind. There would be no confession from me. As he started to leave, I told him I appreciated his helping me watch after her because she was apt to go off her rocker at any time. I told him I thought she needed a complete psychological evaluation.

"Mattie, I designed and built this house and put the tall tin-top roof on it to keep the cats and Mary Ann off of it. I was so afraid that she was going to fall and hurt herself real bad at the other house. Washing dishes is not my cup of tea since my hands are allergic to the dishwashing soap. A woman's place is inside the house, not on top of it."

"Crime Don't Pay"

"Mattie, you have to be careful about the company you keep. I wanted to tell you this story so you can learn how to pick your friends." I made a mistake that almost got me sent to Alcatraz. There was a hometown football game on Friday night, and to celebrate the victory we made plans to have a watermelon party. The plans did not include any financial arrangements to pay for the watermelons, and no one in the group offered to bankroll the party. Things took a wrong turn when someone said he knew the location of a watermelon patch on Snake Ridge west of Baskin, Louisiana. This community is sometimes referred to by the more elite residents living there as Reptile Heights. I wondered how I got caught up in this group. I must have been kidnapped by this bunch of thugs who looked as if they had apprenticed with Al Capone, Robin Hood, or some other notorious gangster. Before I knew what was happening, I was in the back of the truck going too fast to jump out with more than a football team on a criminal mission. Myles Harper "Duffy" McDuffie was the driver of his father's 1949 dark green pickup truck, which he had previously flipped bottom side up on a gravel road and not bent a fender. The boys referred to him as the "Getaway Man" because he was lead-footed and drove fast. The moon was shining brightly, and watermelons were glistening everywhere begging to be eaten. After swiping a truckload of melons, Thunderfoot McDuffie began to nurse truck and boys home to friendly territory on tires as slick as a maypop. The law did not need to catch us with our loot on the side of the road with a flat. Somebody said that God doesn't hear sinners, but we prayed anyway that He would help us in our getaway.

We arrived safely back at Mr. Myles McDuffie's service station and sat under the canopy and ate watermelons until our bellies looked like a pregnant girl's. This relatively quiet town had long been asleep when we decided to get rid of all the evidence. We cleaned up the remnants and rinds of the watermelons and put them into the truck to carry for disposal. Duffy drove to the north end of town and turned right into the Cities Service Station operated by Mr. Pie Russell. The tall steep green roof was an inviting place to hurl a rind, and I could envision a spectacular crash as it slid off the roof. A big disappointment took place. Standing in the back of a moving truck is unstable, and one's balance is hard to maintain. I picked a large portion of rind that was wet with juice to entertain us with the physical law of gravity providing the impetus. At the moment I heaved the rind, the truck swerved, and the rind slipped out of my hand and went crashing through the front beveled window. The judge and the jury in the back of the truck thought I had done this malicious deed on purpose. Nothing could have been further from the truth; it was surely an accident. We all agreed that we would never tell any of the happenings of this night, secrets that we would carry to our graves. To assure our silence, we took an old Indian blood oath that would bind us as brothers. A sharp knife cut each of us at the first digit on our index finger, and the code of silence sealed by the blood mingled between all of us. We threw the rest of the watermelon parts off of the low water bridge on Bayou Macon at Crockett Point. We scattered like a covey of quail and all went home.

My father rousted me from a deep sleep on Saturday morning at 9:30 to announce that someone was here to see me. I begged him to let me sleep a little longer, but he demanded I get up because it was an important visitor. When he said it was the sheriff, I nearly jumped through the roof. Have you ever asked a question and already knew the answer? "What does he want?" I asked. "He just wants to ask you some questions," Dad said. I knew this conversation was not going to be good because I did not have time to rehearse.

Hiram Waller, a well-known fiddle player known as "Sweet Cake", was the Sheriff of Franklin Parish. He was a man small in stature, about five feet five and one-half inches tall from the top of his bald head to his shoe soles, but he was a noted big crime solver. As he clutched my arm, he escorted me from our front porch and seated me on the passenger side in the back seat of the car. He slowly sat down in the driver's seat of the big black sedan, put his arm on the back of the seat, and then faced me. "Son, do you know anything about a watermelon party last night?" he said. "Yes, sir," was my reply. "Would you like to tell me about it?" he asked. Not really I thought, but I knew this answer would not satisfy him, so I planned a new strategy. I would tell him as little as I could. "Well, son, I'm waiting," he said. I told him we ate some watermelons at

Mr. Myles McDuffie's service station to celebrate the football game victory Friday night. "Who all were present?" he asked. I told him that I did not think they called roll and it was so dark I did not recognize everyone there. "Do you know anything about a watermelon rind being thrown through Mr. Pie Russell's window at the Cities Service Station?" he asked. "No, sir," I answered. "Are you sure?" he countered. "Yes, sir, I am," I stammered. Then he said, "Son, do you know what they do to boys who do criminal damage to people's property?" He explained to me that they would take a guilty boy away from his parents and put him in the middle of San Francisco Bay on an island called Alcatraz. He said the boy would never get to see his parents again and that no one had ever escaped from that horrible place. Over and over again he asked me if I knew anything. My reply was always, "No, sir." Then he said, "If you don't know anything, you would not mind if we prosecuted the guilty one responsible for this criminal damage, would you?" I said that I thought the one who had done this deed ought to be held accountable.

The blood oath and the code of silence gave me confidence that this secret would go with us to our graves. I had exhibited a great deal of strength and composure under the pressure of questioning. The sheriff looked at me through those beady eyes and said, "Son, the Louisiana State Police Crime Lab is on the way up here to get the fingerprints off that watermelon rind." Knowing my prints were on that rind, nothing I could do would stop the spasms in my legs as my knees banged together. These rigors I was going through probably testified of my guilt. "Son, are you sure you don't know who destroyed the man's property?" I took the biggest chance in my life and gambled that the crime lab unit would have a crash and not get here to run the fingerprint test, and, with a lump in my throat that was about to choke me, I said, "No, sir."

He cranked the car and said, "Let's go to town." I could have thrown a rock from my house to the middle of the village. I could sense that he was not going to take me to buy an R.C. Cola and a Moon Pie. Like a martin flying to her gourd, he drove straight to Mr. Myles McDuffie's Service Station. We drove up to the gas pumps, and there stood two of my blood oath brothers on the raised portion with their feet sticking over. Both of them pointed at the same time and said, "You've got your man."

A blood oath does not mean a thing if someone turns up enough heat. The High Sheriff used the same tactics when he talked to Myles Harper "Duffy" McDuffie. The sheriff knew he was at a crime scene when he saw all the watermelon seeds. He then went to Danny Donnell's house, and Mr. Ernest, Danny's dad, delivered him to the sheriff for questioning. The stories the sheriff heard from these two snitches quickly developed leaks. He put both of them in the black sedan and told them the story about Alcatraz and that it may be their home for the rest of their lives. The sheriff knew all the answers to the questions he asked me before coming to my house. They had given me up! He did not seem to care if this ordeal had stunted my growth or nearly caused me to have a heart attack.

"Mattie Grace, this one event did more to break up my life of crime than anything. It nearly destroyed my taste for watermelon, and I learned that most people are not willing to go to jail for your crime." A sheriff will run for re-election based on his success in solving crimes. He can hire the best detectives and investigators and train them at the best academies, but ninety percent of all crimes are still solved by using a snitch. Maybe the snitch needs a pat on the back and not the sheriff.

The men of Crowville had met at the coffee shop and barbershop to recount and replay the football victory of the night before. Mr. Pie Russell opened the Cities Service Station at daylight to find a mess with glass and watermelon rind on the floor. The news quickly made its way to the coffee tables and checker benches, and the pieces of this puzzle were put together as the real picture began to emerge. Hoping to scare us back toward the straight and narrow, this group of fathers voted to call the sheriff. Boys get so much wax in their ears they do not listen to their fathers. What I began to hear was nearly deafening to me—a father hurt by my behavior leading me down the path of restitution.

I stood before Mr. Pie Russell, a man who worked on a badly crippled leg to make a living, and I apologized and assured him I would pay for all damages. A kind response from this man made me ashamed of my actions even though I meant him no harm. He did not know that the rind had slipped out of my hand, even though it did look like a malicious act. He was only the proprietor and not the owner of the property. He directed me to the owner of the property, Mr. Robert "Bob" Hammons, who lived just behind the service station. My father drove me over in front of his house, blew the car horn, and said, "You need to talk to him, son." Now Mr. Bob was a sight to make eyes sore. He was a gruff old man with un-kempt hair and a big Roman nose as big as your fist that was plastered with varicose veins, and he spoke in a gravelly voice. He walked out on the porch dressed in a pair of seersucker pants, a small-strapped T-shirt, and suspenders. An ugly sight appeared on the porch as he rolled up his lips showing his gums, looked at me, and said, "Boy, what do you want?" I thought I might need a bracer of whiskey to be able to tell him. I felt like Jell-O. I explained what he already knew about the happenings of the past night, but he wanted to hear the confession from me.

"Mattie, I felt like a rat caught in a trap. Here I was at Mr. Hammon's mercy, and all I wanted was to get out of the trap." I told Mr. Bob that my hand had done the damage, but that my heart did not mean it, and that it was an accident that I would pay for. He looked over my head past where I stood and said in a gruff voice, "A.J., this boy is in trouble, and I think we'll put him in jail. The place to curb crime is in the high chair, not the electric chair. Take him to jail," he said as he slammed the front door in my face. My screams and pleas for a second chance were ignored. "Mattie, I didn't know at the time, but old man Bob Hammons should have won an academy award for playing his role in the watermelon saga!" He dang near scared me out of my skin. The men of our town were probably proud they had a part in ridding our village of crime. They had many laughs at our expense when they told this story.

"Mattie, I learned early, crime don't pay!"

Old People Can Solve Puzzles

"Mattie, sometimes what you see is not what you get. This is especially true with old people." Some of them are not as dumb as they look. There can be a lot of rich soil under the snow, and there

139

can be a lot of smarts under gray hair. They have a sixth sense when it comes to sniffing out the truth. The highlight of our year was when my brother Jerry and I got to spend two weeks during the summer recess from school with our paternal grandparents. Grandmother Collier always had a cupboard full of teacakes and cookies to feed a hungry boy. The little sawmill town of Atlanta, Louisiana, twelve miles south of Winnfield, left an indelible country flavored accent on my life. We milked the cows, churned the butter, picked the peas, dug the potatoes, slopped the hogs, and drew up the drinking water from the well that we put into a bucket on the back porch. It was so refreshing as we drank water from a gourd dipper.

Annie Lee Collier and Aunt Nettie Neal were sisters who came from the Ferguson clan. My grandmother married Marion Franklin Collier (Mr. M.F.), and Aunt Nettie married Joe Neal. "Mattie, trying to learn about our past is like following footprints in windblown snow. As we follow them, time seems to erase them. We finally arrive at a place and realize they are gone. Mattie, I wanted you to know something about my past." Two boys will take the bark off of anybody's tree and erode the patience of someone with nerves of steel. The bond between two sisters can be strong enough that words do not have to be spoken. They can tell what each other is thinking. Granny Collier would send a care package with us to Aunt Nettie's and Uncle Joe's so that they could experience the joy of learning from us. I think now that we were swapped around to help all of them preserve their sanity.

We gathered the neighborhood boys, chose up sides, and played cowboys and Indians. It was hard to find feathers on the yard to make the Indian headbands. The feathers had to come from Aunt Nettie's laying hens and a few roosters. Bright boys have cognitive abilities that can quickly solve problems. We used a No. 3 washtub from the back porch as a trap. We used a forked stick to prop the washtub up under the deck of the front porch and tied a string to the stick. After crumbling some leftover cornbread under the tub, we hid behind the chimney and waited for the chickens to enter the trap. Once the chickens were caught, we took them outback by the smokehouse and removed their feathers for our headbands. The chickens yelled bloody murder when we pulled feathers from their wings and tails.

They would not come to the nest to lay while we were on the premises. Egg production fell off to nearly nothing, and the yard was full of chickens with missing feathers. Looking at the evidence, Aunt Nettie threatened to take us to the peach orchard if our behavior did not stop. The anatomy of boys makes it nearly impossible for them to remember things tomorrow that they were told today. Aunt Nettie promised a whipping if these things occurred tomorrow. "Mattie, boys were made with two ears, and when they go to sleep at night the things they heard today fall through their heads and are left on the pillow when they get up the next morning. A cork stopper could be placed in the ear next to the pillow to prevent this loss."

The next morning the boys could not remember where they had placed their Indian headbands, and they set out to make more. They trapped four chickens under the No. 3 washtub and carried them to the smokehouse to sacrifice their feathers. The pain to extract the wing feathers seemed to be greater than the pain with pulling the tail feathers. The terrifying sounds of chicken pain traveled from the smokehouse to Aunt Nettie's ears. She yelled, "Are you boys fooling with my chickens?" Then again, "Are you boys fooling with my chickens?" She was close enough to have smelled us by this time. With the exception of one, all the chickens were dropped, and they all looked like bottle rockets when they scattered. My brother Jerry still held a big Dominecker hen behind his back next to the dug well. As soon as Aunt Nettie's bonnet appeared at the corner of the smokehouse, Jerry dropped the old hen into the well, and Aunt Nettie saw nothing. She joined the Indian part of this uprising, went on the warpath, and lined us up single file in the peach orchard. A time of reckoning was going to take place for every one of us. "Mattie, the one who brings us to the final reckoning will already know all of the answers to the questions we will be asked." Aunt Nettie had us follow her to the front porch and poured each of us a glass of grape Kool-Aid, set us on the steps, and began to point out some obvious things. She pointed to a Rhode Island Red hen, a wing feather missing from her right wing and two feathers missing from her tail. "Boys, is anybody wearing those feathers?" she asked. She pointed next to a big White Rock hen with a feather missing on both wings and one tail feather gone. One of the boys sitting on the steps could not hide his involvement. A colorful game rooster came strutting across the yard looking like he had been run over by a freight train. Three wing feathers were missing on the port side, two were missing on the starboard side, and all his tail feathers were gone. Three boys were wearing headbands that were picked up at the site of the train wreck. "Mattie, why is it easier to tell a lie than the truth? There was no train wreck."

Three days later Uncle Joe Neal went to draw a bucket of water from the well by dropping the bucket with the flapper on a rope into the well. When he pulled the plunger on the bucket from the well, the bucket for the porch filled with chicken feathers. What was down in the well was now making its way up in the bucket.

"Mattie, old people are good at solving puzzles because they were once a piece of the puzzle."

Chapter 14

DOG, PONY, AND HOG SHOWS

I n this day and age, the simple things of life seem to have lost their appeal. The things we cut our teeth on just do not cut it anymore. People have an insatiable appetite and hunger that can only be fed and satisfied by the extraordinary.

"Mattie, there is a game called keeping up with the Joneses, but sometimes it can be called the rat race. The dog and pony shows of life keep us constantly jumping through hoops. The trend today is to outdo our neighbors and to impress our friends." I told Mattie the story of King Solomon and the Queen of Sheba. When the Queen heard of the wisdom and prosperity of King Solomon, she came a long way to see if the reports were true. As the visit concluded, they both exchanged gifts that were virtually a swap—gold, silver, ivory, and spices. However, near the end of the visit, King Solomon played his trump card and took her to the ape and peacock show. Rare exhibits that no one else had, these animals had come on a boat from Tarshish. The Queen of Sheba rode a long way on a camel just to see an ape and a peacock (II Chronicles 9:1-21). "Mattie," I said, "a peacock has the ugliest legs I ever saw, and an ape can be as obnoxious as one's mother-in-law. If the Queen was impressed with this show, no one recorded it."

The intoxicating demand and frenzy to have more have become addictive in my lifetime. Because we are not satisfied with simple and ordinary things in life anymore, we indulge in excesses that have imprisoned us and made us slaves. Once we feed the fire to be different, we spend the rest of our lives gathering the wood to feed the fire. The fuel to feed the fire is very likely growing the debt of the average family. People are living above their means. Earlier in my life, my father was also my banker. I always seemed to need more money and never had enough. I was never bashful and often asked him for more. He was not bashful either. He knew how to say "no," sometimes loud enough to hurt my ears, as he asked if I thought he were a money tree. I answered him by saying that I knew that he was not a money tree, but it would be all right with me if he just wrote a check for these necessary funds. The professor in him fervently delivered a lecture that often ended in these words, "Boy, it is not the high cost of living that's killing you. It's the cost of high living." Today the prevailing philosophy is to spend more than we make and to throw the idea of saving for a rainy day out the window.

"Mattie, I can remember when I was a boy the Ringling Brothers and Barnum and Bailey Circus came to our area." Billed as *The Greatest Show on Earth,* it arrived in town on sixty railroad cars. It was a three-ring circus under the big top with sideshows as added attractions. The glitz and glamour could sure open a country boy's eyes and keep him spellbound with tricks and magic everywhere. Parents splurged and spent money that was hard to come by in those days to take their children to see this spectacle. The price of tickets for admission was outlandish and exorbitant and left pockets drained to nearly dry. Once we get started jumping through hoops, the cost of the dog and pony shows just keeps going up. This subtle approach reminds me of someone who steals a cow and brings it to his barn and continues to steal the milk. " Look! Here come the balloons, the peanuts, the popcorn, and the cotton candy. Look again! Our money is leaving with the clowns that frisked us and drained our pockets." The circus always costs more than we think it will, and so will dog and pony shows.

Sometimes I have a brainstorm. My brainstorms can be considered dangerous because some folks think I am not wrapped too tight anyway. They know that I am crazy when I tell them I am the milkman's boy. I told Mattie about one particular brainstorm that was going to make me rich. If my plan worked, I was going to be on the receiving end of a lot of money. I was going to swap Mattie for a "skit monkey" and take my saxophone and accordion, get on a street corner, play music while this monkey entertained the crowd, and then frisk people out of their money. Some people spend their lives chasing rainbows. After I told the story, I apologized to Mattie Grace and told her that all the money in the world could not buy her from me. I loved her too much. She just wagged her tail.

The new philosophy of economy embraced by our leaders is to spend ourselves out of debt. They believe that, if we throw enough money at a problem, we can fix it. The growing debt in both the public and private sectors, if left unchecked, will lead us to a major wreck. Will we, or can we, survive the crash? It is hard to sit by and watch the sick patient be neglected until he has to be put on life support. The vital signs of our nation are critical.

A poor man trying to play a rich man's game and living beyond his means has hurt a lot of poor men. "Mattie, they say you can't choose your kinfolks, but you can choose your friends." I heard some men talking about Bubba, the southern redneck, the other day, and the story sounded really familiar. These people said Bubba had just bought one of those new souped-up trucks with loud pipes and big mud grip tires jacked way up in the air. He had a gun rack with a new shotgun and deer rifle behind the seat in the window. Somebody said he traded in his old single-barrel for the new shotgun because the old piece of junk would not look right in a new truck. A new matching red Honda 4X4 ATV that was woods- ready with racks and accessories was in the back cargo space. The more I heard, the more I felt this was not the Bubba I knew. The Bubba I knew was always poor, but nobody worked harder to make a living for his wife and four kids. Hauling pulpwood was hard work, and his income was dependent on the weather. When it was dry, he had to save for a rainy day. I was shocked when I saw the truck at the NAPA store. It had a chrome grill and winch guard, headache racks filled with running lights, and signs on the rear window – BUBBA'S RIDE along with his National Rifle Association sticker and his hunting club membership. I wondered if Bubba had robbed the bank. When I thought more about it, I decided he very well could have, one way or the other. A person may not be kin to Bubba by blood, but he can be kin by actions. The guys at the coffee shop and the barbershop said they thought Bubba must have found a gold mine, but I thought it was a bit more likely that he had built a whiskey still. I hope the revenuers do not catch him because his babies need a daddy.

One day Bubba flagged Mattie and me down, flashing his lights and blowing his horn. He wanted to know what we thought about his new rides. Mattie and I got out of the truck to talk to him. I asked him about his wife Marie and their children and about their welfare. "Do you have any life insurance to take care of them if a tree falls on you in the woods?" I asked. I dropped a bomb on him when I told him how much I spent to send my son to college and medical school and how it wrecked my finances. "Do you have a ton of money hid somewhere to send your tribe to school?" I asked. There are bunches of people who do not know what a nest egg is, and Bubba was one of them. A nest egg is like a savings account, the one we have in reserve that we leave in the nest to encourage others to be laid in the nest. Bubba looked at me as if this thought just flew right over his head. I knew that I was going to have to get closer to the ground down on his level to talk to him about economics. Later on that day, I told Mattie, "It is hard for some people to grasp the matter of managing money." I never had much money to practice with; therefore, it has taken me a lot longer to learn than the average bear. I am still not an expert, but I thought I would drop some hints and aimed low enough so that Bubba could get a hold of them. "Mattie, pay attention, because someone is sure to put you to the test."

I explained to Bubba that appreciation is the term to be used when something you buy increases in value and is worth more than you paid for it. Depreciation is the decrease in value when something that is bought is not worth what was paid for it. Collateral is often a matter of dispute because it depends on determining what something is worth. If a banker uses collateral to secure a loan, it is never worth what a borrower thinks it is. I continued to tell Bubba about budgets, profit and loss, capital gains, balance sheets, and net worth. I wondered if any of this information had soaked into his head. He just stood there and looked out into space as if all of this had made no sense. Bubba looked at me and said, "All I wanted to know is what you thought about my rides."

I guess that most people do not care what we think about their rides, or how much they spend on dog and pony shows, or how much money they throw away on luxuries, or how much they waste as they indulge in excesses. Often the opinions of others are unwanted and unwelcomed. I think it best to let every man paddle his own boat. We can bargain with a man who needs a life jacket.

"Mattie, dog and pony shows are a lot like beauty contests." Many contestants or participants enter, but ultimately only one finishes at the top. Everyone who enters a contest dreams of being a winner once she has strutted her stuff before a panel of judges. Finishing at the top is just about as likely as winning the lottery. All are losers but one. Being the second place finisher is like kissing a sister, and there is not much satisfaction in that. If someone chooses to run with the big dogs, fast horses, and pretty girls, he enters high maintenance territory, and this lifestyle requires a lot of money. Show dogs do not get to roll in the dirt; fast horses never get out of a stall to eat grass; and beautiful women do not like to wash dishes. People have gone stark raving mad on the amount of time and money they spend in the pursuit of things that become old and are later abandoned. Sometimes these are referred to as merely fads. Money for the dog shows, pony shows, and beauty pageants can eat a poor boy's nest egg up at the drop of a hat. Horse trailers, trucks to pull them, dog palaces and houses, saddles and tack, evening gowns, party dresses, swimsuits, hairdos, groomers, trainers, chauffeurs, and worn out mothers and fathers who cheered at the shows all add to the bill.

I told Mattie Grace, "My father used to make a remark that stuck with me when he said some people are too big for their britches. I think he was talking about people who were big shots. All I ever wanted to be was a good shot. Mattie, you remember when we went to the groomer to get your hair prettied up for St. Patrick's Day and met that woman with the high-dollar dog?" She acted like a big shot when she asked me, "What kind of dog is that?" Before I could tell her Mattie was the best dog in the world, the smart aleck answered her own question and said, "I bet it's a schnorkie." I told Mattie, "She was just pointing out that you were a half breed and probably worthless." I was afraid to spit on the ground for fear that my spit would catch the grass on fire. However, goodness overcame me as I pitied her husband and wondered if he were hen-pecked. Standing by a long black Mercedes, she was dressed as if she had been to a Vogue Magazine fashion shoot with her finger nails manicured and exotically painted, her face kissed with the proper shades of blush and lipstick, and her cute little dog on the end of a fashion leash. I took a good look at her, but I did not see any tattoos on her. Not because I had any interest in her, but just to make conversation I asked her, "What kind of little dog is that?" The door opened quickly, and I got an ear full of all the details and history of this little rare Yorkie. As I listened to this braggadocio, I thought she was its grandmother instead of its mother. She paid $4,200.00 for this thing that was supposed to be of a rare color, and it looked like it had syrup poured all over it. I would never have known how much Mattie was worth if I had not run into this woman and dog. I would not swap Mattie for a trainload of dogs like that. Maybe I need to get somebody to help me figure up what I am worth. After that encounter, I escorted Mattie all over town to show off her new hairdo, bow and matching St. Patrick's scarf, and green painted toe nails because I was so proud of her.

It takes a different budget to feed one's wants instead of one's needs. The generation of my parents and grandparents struggled to provide for the basic needs of their families. The bare necessities were wrangled by hard work and determination in the days of the depression and the dust bowl. The pioneering spirit of the American people began to knock on the door of opportunity driving westward expansion and industrial growth. Somewhere and somehow along the way, the appetite of most of us has changed from our needs to our wants. The wish and want lists are never satisfied and always continue to increase. When we grow tired of the things we have accumulated, we decide to bury them. The graveyard for wish and want things is called a rummage sale. The fire that burns to want more is never satisfied because the list is extensive and endless. Coin collections, stamp collections, gun collections, art collections, automobile collections, bass boats, fast cars, jewelry, cruises, vacations, safaris, along with a thousand other pursuits, fill the want lists of many. Remember that we will have to gather the wood to feed the fire of things we want. Once we get on a treadmill, it is hard to get off.

The dog shows, pony shows, and hog shows of today were unheard of when I was a barefoot boy and had no shoes. My wardrobe never changed during the first five years I went to school. My school pictures from first through fifth grade were taken in a pair of Tuff Nut carpenter overalls bought from Mr. Lee McDuffie's store in downtown Crowville, Louisiana. There was no uptown Crowville, and there is still none today. In the overall scheme of things, I think we could be considered to be Rural Free Delivery (RFD). Many community schools had 4-H clubs and Future Farmer of America (FFA) clubs with programs that benefited many children and families and strengthened the self-sufficiency of the family. Young people learned to be responsible, productive, and self sufficient through livestock shows where cattle, horses, sheep, goats, chickens, rabbits, and other farm animals were raised and shown. The animals that were not best of breed, best of show, champion or reserve champion ended up as culls on the dinner table. I believe we should not get very far from this way of life because our past could come to visit us again. If it does, I would not be surprised to see a lot of cow, horse, and chicken thieves show up since many people would not know how to survive in this environment.

"Mattie, just as there are dog and pony shows, there are also other shows." People should never pass up a modern hog show. I guarantee it will knock their socks off, blow their skirts up, boggle their minds, and open their eyes. Hog pens are filled with Fat Boys, Crossbones, Fat Bobs, Road Kings, Nightrains, Soft Tails, Street Glides, V-rods, Deuces, Ultra Glides, Heritage Classics, Rocker C's, Wide Glides and other Harley Davidson breeds. People who get caught up in the herd mentality then want to be part of the gang. We need to be careful of wolves in sheep's clothing that infiltrate the hog pen.

The man that throws his hat into this ring and decides to run with the big dogs will have to get up off of his hip pockets. Bubba will have to cut a lot of pulpwood to get into this game. The entry fees and dues to participate are not to be sneezed at. The price of a Harley Hog can exceed the cost of a new Cadillac, not considering the accessories and add-ons. The add-ons on a motorcycle can easily surpass the price of a country boy's mule. Poor boys get thrown by mules, some more than once, and rich dudes get thrown by motorcycles. Because there is a tremendous difference in the price of the accessories to outfit a mule rider and a motorcycle rider, one can quickly tell which one is which. It is hard for me to paint a word picture of what one of these hog boys looks like, but if we follow the noise and catch up to one we can see for ourselves.

I loved watching the expression on Mattie's face when we met the hog herders on the roads we traveled. The hog herders we saw were decked out in leather pants or chaps, a leather coat or vest, leather gloves and boots, a crash helmet and goggles, and a big leather billfold and chain that once held a lot of money. All of this motorcycle garb and paraphernalia have been purchased on the premise that it may prevent road rash when, not if, a crash occurs. Since wrecks occur, especially with my mule Willie, perhaps I should invest in a used football uniform with shoulder pads, rib pads, kneepads, thigh pads, hip pads, and headgear. The difference between mule garb and motorcycle garb is that I can get a used football uniform for a little of nothing at a rummage sale, and it will protect me in the next mule wreck. "Mattie, I hope Willie will recognize me in the football suit and not think I am a scarecrow! Mule garb consists of straw hats, overalls, and used football suits."

The allure of the Harley Davidson hog rallies draws more people to Sturgis, Four Corners, Daytona, and other places than evangelistic rallies anywhere. People from all walks of life including doctors, lawyers, politicians, bankers, farmers, business people, construction workers, truckers, engineers, college professors, pharmacists, and a host of others join this wave. Old blood, bad blood, new blood, and shed blood have been a part of this culture for a long time. We can see the story of the good, the bad, and the ugly.

A new day is dawning in this little hamlet where I live. Mattie and I witnessed the changes every day. The mule culture is fast becoming extinct and being replaced by roads full of hogs. The peace and quiet is expelled by the noise of these new iron horses. With all this noise, the hearing aid business ought to begin to flourish here. New opportunities are just around the corner. A new breed of bikers—bishops, elders, evangelists, preachers, deacons, and church members—may saturate this culture with good that can overcome the bad and the ugly. Which sounds better—Satan's Tramps or Satisfied Saints, Hell's Angels or Heaven's Hosts as groups in the new turf wars? This church bunch justifies their entrance into the hog culture by saying they can evangelize the world on a Harley faster than from the back of a donkey. Really?

The real challenge for any of us is changing the world and not letting the things of the world change us. There is a saying that if it looks like a duck, walks like a duck, swims like a duck, and quacks like a duck, it must be a duck. There are a lot of churches that get caught up in dog, pony, and hog shows that change us. Old-time religion is no longer good enough for us. Maybe we ought to run the puppets out of the church instead of the preacher. Maybe we ought to throw the amplifiers into the yard and rebuild our altars, and maybe our bickering could lead to our brokenness. Our culture leads our churches to join in the dog and pony show mentality by having extravagant services and big productions that appeal to crowds. Churches have created a circus atmosphere to entertain us instead of edifying us. We used to come and sing "I Stand Amazed;" now we come and sit amused. It is hard at a masquerade party to tell who's who when some attend looking like sheep but, under the wool, are actually wolves. God's work has never been done by the many, but by the few, and not by a host, but rather by a handful. Until heavy hearts, broken by the condition of our nation, literally shoulder the load in prayer with pure hearts and lay these petitions down on His altar will He heal our land. The recipe is simple.

I told Mattie that I must march to the beat of a different drummer because things have changed so much in my lifetime that I am out of step with this generation. The world has run off and left me behind, and I have lost my desire to keep up. I will probably die and not have any tattoos or an earring, eyebrow piercing, nose piercing, a tongue stud, or body piercing in other places I have heard about. One of these days people will display some of us in museums like dinosaurs and laugh at us as relics of the past. No specimens from my past evolved with earrings, eyebrow piercings, tongue studs, nose studs, body piercings, or tattoos. This kind of behavior would have got us shot when I was boy. I am disgusted to see young girls and beautiful women mutilate and disfigure their bodies in defiance of their parents and society. The rock culture and the Hollywood crowd influence young people. These influences are by the same people who mutilate the Star Spangled Banner or forget the words when they sing before national audiences. I hope these stars can con enough people out of their hard earned money to take some singing lessons to support their extravagant lifestyles. Even though I have been embarrassed by their singing and acting, they will not get a dime of my money for their lessons. I remember when I told the people, "You ain't seen nothing yet," and now that we have seen, I asked Mattie, "How long will it be before you say enough is enough?"

Chapter 15

LOOK FOR 'EM, WATCH FOR 'EM, GET 'EM

M attie Grace heard these three expressions more than anything else: "look for 'em," "watch for 'em," and "get 'em." I could awaken her from a deep sleep when I said any one of these three phrases, and immediately I would have her undivided attention. She learned quickly what these words meant and what her role was in doing what I wanted. I used "look for 'em" when I wanted to show her something or wanted her to go look for something. Mattie was my constant companion, and I would see things that I thought might be interesting to her. People, dogs, cows, horses, mules, and squirrels would capture her attention.

The coyote prowls of the nighttime were always a threat to our family of pets. Before we went to bed at night, we made a head count before lockdown and the hatches were battened down. Mattie would head the roundup each night before going to bed, looking for family members dictated on the list of the missing. She knew each of our family by name, by sight, and by smell. They could not run or hide from her. We could go to the back porch and say, "Mattie, BooBoo is missing. Remember he is hard to see on a dark night, go look for 'em." The circles of the search would become wider and wider until she found a track, the aroma of BooBoo. He would willingly follow her to the safety of home and leave the rats for another day. "Mattie, Miss Muffin was missing at roll call. Look for 'em." In sniffing Muffin out of hiding, Mattie applied the lesson she learned when she tracked me in the woods. Because of her, Muffin was not coyote bait that night. Our Bach is a magician at catching rats, not a musician that writes concertos, but when he missed roll call, I said, "Look for 'em, Mattie." The search was then on, and it lasted longer than usual. Mattie passed by several times as she looked in all the familiar places. I became afraid that a pack of coyotes had got Bach and we would never see him again. Then north of the house near the grown-up thicket, Mattie began to bark as though she was calling for me to come see; she was pleading for help. With the spotlight in hand, I found her standing near Bach who had a huge field rat in his clutches. I am glad the balance of nature bunch was not there because I had to promise Bach I would get a taxidermist to mount his trophy before I could get him to give it up. We all went to the house to show Mary Ann the prize.

"Watch for 'em" was the term I used when I wanted Mattie to be extra vigilant like a soldier or a sentry. An old man needs a young dog. Too many high powered gunshots, too many hours sitting in crop dusters behind radial engines, too many screaming turbochargers on farm tractors, too many loud noises on oil field drilling rigs, and too many brain tumors have left me deaf in one ear and nearly deaf in the other. If I lost my glasses, I would probably starve to death because I could not read the menu at the café. I called Mattie my hearing ear dog and my seeing eye dog. I believed she could hear a redbug walking in the grass, and she would look in the direction of any sound she heard. Since I do not have bi-lateral hearing, I could not course a sound, and I depended on Mattie for this service. When I said "watch for 'em," watch for 'em she would, not taking her eyes off what she was watching and not even charging overtime. She stood her watch with great faithfulness.

Many times in life we need to open our eyes before making decisions. Many times we can make the right choices just by watching or looking. I was Mattie's philosophy coach, and she was always head and shoulders above Bubba in understanding the look for 'em, watch for 'em, before getting 'em philosophy. The many consequences of bad decisions we make can cripple us in life, and some can even kill us. Mattie and I were between Baskin, Louisiana, and

Winnsboro, Louisiana, on Highway 15 in the southbound lane, and she was fast asleep. A car in front of us was driving erratically, running off the shoulder to the right, into and across the fast lane on the left. I yelled, "Look for 'em," and as fast as I could snap my fingers, Mattie saw what I saw, and I said "Watch for 'em" to alert her that we might see a bad wreck. I thought the driver must be a drunk, but most drunks drive better than this. The car went forty miles per hour, then seventy-five miles per hour; it traveled back and forth across both lanes at forty and then eighty. "Watch for 'em, Mattie," I said. Then I recorded the license plate number and started to pass the car. Oblivious to the fact that anyone else was in the world, a woman was driving with both knees on the steering wheel and texting with both hands on a cell phone. The thought occurred to me that she might be trying to text her boyfriend or husband until I took a good look at her. Then I thought it was more likely that she may still be shopping for one or the other and had become desperate because her time was running out. The more I thought about it, the more certain I was that she was not texting her children either because I doubted she was smart enough to know how to conceive. I finally passed her in front of the Franklin Cotton Warehouse and turned into the parking lot of Sullivan's Feed Store. I looked in the rearview mirror to see this woman still whacking at the keys on the cell phone when she stopped parallel to my passenger side door. "Get 'em, Mattie," I said. Mattie started barking and biting at the window as I lowered it enough for Mattie to be heard. The woman got out of her car and said, "What's wrong with that little dog? Will it bite?" When I told Mattie to sit, she quietly got into my lap and acted like a little lamb. I told the woman, "Mattie was scared and wanted me to tell you something for her." The driver wanted to know if Mattie Grace could talk. I told her no, but that she could think out loud, whatever that meant. I told the woman, "You not only scared Mattie, but you scared me when you nearly ran over us back down the road." Mattie attended the class on Common Sense that I taught to all of our family members. Seeing this woman reminded me of one of the most profound statements I ever heard, the one that came from the old black and white movie featuring John Wayne who said, "There ain't no cure for stupid." I went on to tell the driver, "Lady, Mattie wanted me to tell you she thinks it's stupid to text and drive." Mattie made an A in the course on Common Sense in case this lady might ask.

"Get 'em" could be converted to "sic 'em" in a dog's vernacular. When Mattie heard these words, she knew these were fighting words. People who knew Mattie knew that she would sacrifice every bone in her body to protect me. When everybody picked at her, they were amazed and amused at her grit. If we took up for the Lord with this same fervor, no one would offend Him in our presence. Big dogs and little dogs, cows and calves, mules and men, nothing scared her. Mattie was just a little bundle of fur, but she had a great big heart. The most fitting expression I have heard that could characterize the life of Mattie Grace is, "It is not the size of the dog in the fight; it is rather the size of the fight in the dog."

Look for 'em, watch for 'em, and get 'em are three expressions that each of us needs to hear, not just Mattie. She learned quickly what these things meant and what her role in doing what I wanted was. Our Master has tried to teach us also what these things mean.

Look for 'em is our wakeup call to look for the coming of the Lord. We are not only to look for Him but also for those who are not looking for Him. The search should never end, and the looking for them should never stop. The stories of the lost sheep, the lost coin, and the lost son all had happy endings. All of these celebrations were punctuated with a spirit of joy and rejoicing mixed with gladness and merrymaking, and a funeral for the dead was changed to a festival for the living (Luke 15:3-32).

The call to vigilance requires us to neither slumber nor sleep. The alarm has sounded to watch for 'em. I Peter 5:8 admonishes us, "Be sober, be vigilant, because your adversary, the devil, like a roaring lion walketh about, seeking whom he may devour." The watchmen are called and chosen to sound the alarm when the enemy appears to warn the people of impending danger. The shepherds are called to watch for 'em and to look after the needs of the sheep. This assignment can, and sometimes will, treat a person like a caged bird. Somebody can feed us, entertain us, and put us in the safety of a cage for protection, but we are not our own. We are bought with a price and belong to someone else. One of these days He will open the door to the cage and set us free to fly where we choose. When that happens for me, send my mail to the Big House!

Get 'em was all Mattie needed to hear to know that there was a threat to me. This was serious business to her, and she became the hedge and stood in the gap to secure my safety. She was never unwilling and, without exception, reported for her assignment. The permeating theme and commandment to every church and every believer is go get 'em. This directive is not optional, has eternal consequences if not followed, and is a divine emphatic imperative, as if a voice would shout, "YOU GO GET 'EM!" Multitudes are everywhere, scattered here and there. Some have been waiting for us to come; others may hide and find flimsy excuses why they should not come. Some are nearby, and others are far away. Those He sends He equips, not with excuses, but with confidence that His word will not return void and empty. In every country, in every city, in every town, and in the highways and hedges, people are waiting and expecting us to come. Some will gladly come, others must be compelled to come, and a few may refuse to come. This assignment is called "fishing for men." To be a successful fisherman, we must keep our hooks in the water. Churches and believers always talk about going fishing for men, but it seems all our time is spent in training people how to fish, digging the bait, and getting ready to go. It seems we never go fishing. "Mattie, let's go fishing. We will keep our bait in the water."

Mattie saw and heard a lot of sermons when she rode with me and went with me on trips. I talked out loud to her as if she were my best friend and told her many stories from my past. The memories were reminders of the journey of a common boy who was helped along the way by parents, grandparents, teachers, mentors, neighbors, friends, pastors and other Picker-Uppers. I am a common boy whose life has been anything but common because of the sacrifice of these people. "Mattie, you can wait too long to say thank you to someone who has meant so much to you. The trips we have made to the cemeteries and the walks taken through the headstones have been more for my benefit than yours. Many of my thank yous have been delivered too late. I will cherish my memories as keepsakes in my heart. Telling you these stories will keep them from fading over time. Mattie, before we get into the truck, we need to make one more stop. We have been here before. Mattie Grace, the night my father went to the Big House, I knew that his time to go had come. The cancer had drained the life from his body. I would have gladly taken his place if I could have. I know that my time will also come and that every step I make brings me closer to the Big House. Mattie, I have had a wonderful journey with memories that have blossomed like flowers to decorate the way. The way to the Big House has been a beautiful trip! As I get closer to home, I want to make sure there is no balance due on my account. We all need to leave here with a zero balance. Mattie, I understand that confession is the only way to keep the slate clean."

Chapter 16

CONFESSION IS GOOD FOR THE SOUL

"Mattie Grace, I have always heard that confession is good for the soul. Before I get started to make things right, I hope God doesn't hold things against preachers. People say that preaching to preachers is like preaching to the choir. They also say it is like pouring water on a duck's back because it just runs off and won't soak in. Mattie, when I told you about dog, pony, and hog shows, I think I may have been too harsh in talking about Bubba, the Harley Hog bunch, the Hollywood crowd, big dogs, fast horses, and pretty girls."

I must admit that there have been times that I have gone down the wrong road, fumbled the ball, made the wrong choice, and just goofed up. My confession comes because I too straddled a motorcycle or two and thought about a tattoo. Yep, I thought I did not want one.

One time I flew an airplane to the Monroe, Louisiana, airport to have some maintenance work done on it. Since the sign in the shop read, "Maintenance $40.00 per hour–If you help, it's $80.00 per hour," I decided to borrow Red Boles' old raggedy truck to save some money on the maintenance bill. I found my way to Howard Griffin's Land-O-Toys & Outdoor Marine on South Grand Street in Monroe. This store was billed as the South's largest outboard motor and motorcycle dealership. A brand spanking new model Honda

Goldwing Interstate Motorcycle that was maroon with gold trim sat on the showroom floor. It was just like a monkey got on my back and followed me around that store until he convinced me I had to have that motorcycle. The salesman thought I was joking when I told him I would buy it if he would bring it to the airport since I had to return Mr. Boles` truck. I paid his cab fare back to the showroom.

The trip back to Crowville was most enjoyable until I thought about what my father might say. There is no telling how many times I heard him say, "Boy, I ought to have pulled your head off when you were born. You ain't got a danged bit of sense." Since he was an agriculture major and not an economics major in college, I thought he might not understand how I saved enough money to pay for this thing by not working on my airplane. I reasoned that if Daddy were a little slow to understand, I could get Bubba to explain it to him. Mary Ann, Clayton, and I climbed aboard the motorcycle to go to my parents' house to face the music. I knew it probably was not going to be a tune I wanted to hear, it would not have much harmony in it, and it might hurt my ears as well as my feelings. My father circled this iron horse three or four times before he said, "Y'all go inside." Then he pointed at me and said, "Except you." This exception to the rule meant "y'all less one," which meant me. He said, "If you ever hurt Mary Ann or that baby on that piece of junk, you better hope it kills you because if you have one breath left when I get to the wreck, I'll stomp it out of you."

Then he wanted to know just what in the world I was thinking when I decided to do such a dumb thing. I was not about to admit that I was not thinking. That is when he said something about me and Bubba being just alike. I was not sure whether he meant our ancestry or our actions. I told him that the monkey that got on my back, plus the salesman, plus the money I saved by not working on my airplane, plus the money I could save on gas with this new ride convinced me I needed it. I knew the climate was not right to talk to him about the economics of this decision; appreciation, depreciation, and collateral were too deep for his comprehension. Besides, Bubba may explain it better where the economics would make more sense to my father. As he walked off, I heard him mumble something about a beer budget and a champagne taste and some idiot splurging on a motorcycle with a bicycle budget.

Simple plans for a spring day on the first Saturday in April found Mary Ann, Clayton, and me on our way to the Enterprise Hills north of Harrisonburg, Louisiana. We rode the Goldwing from Winnsboro, via Louisiana Highway 4, then by Long Lake, and Governor John J. McKeithen's home and farm, past Sandy Bayou Baptist Church to Duty Ferry, where the state-run ferry carried us across the Ouachita River. From there we went to the Chalk Hills to look for sharks' teeth that were deposited there millions of years ago. I had been on field trips to this place many times with the geology department of Northeast Louisiana University, where I learned about this special place. My son accused me of hiding the teeth that we found and scoffed at the idea that the oceans had once covered this site. I showed him that the Bible said that the water covered <u>all</u> the mountains. Some people will argue with a sign and will not believe it even though they see it in black and white. On this gorgeous spring day, our family had smelt the aroma of fresh plowed earth, looked at gardens of flowers, watched newborn calves at play, seen dogwoods that decorated the forest with blooms, and felt close to the One who made it all. As we ate our lunch, we watched a bee gather her nectar, and I thought how sweet it is. God Things seemed to be everywhere.

We came out of the hills near where Bayou Dan runs into the Ouachita River and turned toward Enterprise, past the Duty Ferry Crossing to a sign that read, "New Ouachita Baptist Church." I was scheduled to preach revival services there in three weeks. The church with a steeple sat about a quarter of a mile off the main road. Since I had never been there before, I decided that Mary Ann, Clayton, and I would have a look. Riding the motorcycle in front of the church, I noticed a man and woman next door working in the flowerbeds, and I had a suspicion that I was seeing the pastor and his wife. I would call this an educated guess since he was working with a necktie dangling from his neck and she was politely assisting. Nevertheless, I blew the horn to get his attention, which I already had, and I spoke in a voice as country as I could muster. "Sir, could you tell me where the preacher of this here church lives?" I asked. With a lump in his throat, he confessed to being the pastor, and he wanted to know if he could help me. "Yes sir, when is your next deacons' meeting?" I asked. Since there was not one scheduled that he knew of, he asked again if he could help.

I explained to him that I was coming to preach their revival in three weeks, I was three months behind on my motorcycle note, and it would be repossessed on Tuesday if something were not done. I requested that he talk to the deacons to see if they could make me an advance on my love offering to catch up the notes. I told him that if this help was not possible, then someone would have to come get me and take me home each night after the service. From the expression on his face, I thought a light breeze might blow him away. He made a promise that he would let me know as soon as possible.

Brother Jack Crews only knew me by reputation. His church people who had heard me preach on many occasions had asked him to invite me. Folks who have known me for many years are aware that God has blessed the work of my hands to make a living, a sort of tentmaker like Paul, so that churches are not burdened with our care. Brother Jack did not know that my story was a hoax and that I would leave with none of their money.

After talking to Brother Crews that day, we mounted the motorcycle to continue our trip toward home. Before we got to the main road, Mary Ann said she could not believe I told that man what I did. I said I could hardly believe it either. She begged me to go back and tell him the truth, but I told her he would know soon enough. Traveling south of the church along the Ouachita River, we came to the home of longtime friends, James and Prue Hutchins. James was the song leader and a deacon of New Ouachita Baptist Church. I confessed to James about dropping this bomb on Brother Jack Crews. I told him I was wondering if we needed to defuse it before it blew up. The plot was sure to thicken as more people entered the picture to solve a problem that did not even exist. This story was like a nightmare that is not real.

Before I could get the sugar into my coffee, the telephone rang. Prue announced to James that the Reverend Jack Crews needed to speak to him. Since I could only hear one side of the conversation, I strongly suspected I was the subject of this chatter. James announced that the reverend would be here pronto and that I needed to hide the motorcycle out of sight behind the house. We pushed it to its hiding place and returned to the living area. The doorbell rang, and in walked an unsuspecting victim of a prank. When he looked at me, his face paled as if he saw a ghost. My wife told him he had her permission to assault me for this kind of humor. She apologized for all of our family for my behavior. Laughter is like a medicine, and we did a lot of healing as we finished drinking coffee and building friendships around memories of stories none of us would likely ever forget.

"Mattie, the Bible says we will be judged for every idle word we speak. Idle speaking and idle thinking afflict far too many of us as we rush to feed the wants that lead to our excesses. Mattie, there are two kinds of people in the world, givers and takers. Those that are givers will always be givers, and those that are takers will always be takers. The difference is a matter of the heart." A giver's life is characterized by unselfish acts of benevolence, and a taker's life is marked by a selfish spirit evidenced by greed. A giver chooses to leave things better than he found them, and a taker cares not how he leaves them. "Mattie, do you know why dogs bury bones? For tomorrow. I never thought enough of tomorrow, and there are not enough bones buried in my yard, should I ever need them."

Somebody said the difference between a man and a boy is the price of his toys. This motorcycle was one of many toys I sat on while I was trying to keep up with the Joneses. On multiple occasions, it very nearly got me a plot in the Jones' family cemetery. I have buried several people who were killed in motorcycle accidents. I remember a day not long after I bought the Goldwing. I was riding as an auxiliary deputy with Louisiana State Trooper Danny "Dink" Warner when we were dispatched to an accident involving a motorcycle and an automobile. The motorcyclist had the right-of-way on a state highway when an old man pulled out in front of him causing the wreck. The young man was thrown on top of the hood, over the windshield, across the top onto the trunk, then onto the road. He landed in a seated position with his bottom and shoes sliding down the blacktop road. The friction ate the flesh off of his bones and the soles off of his shoes, another case of someone being buried who had the right of way. After seeing this flash of road rash, I fashioned a "For Sale" sign for my motorcycle. It sold before I could ride it off a diving board like Evel Knievel. I had put less than half of the 4,800 miles on the odometer. People who borrowed it put on the rest. As a result, I took a lesson in depreciation. My daddy was proud of me.

"Mattie Grace, I guess when people stand on the sidelines and watch some of the decisions we make, they think we are crazy. We don't have the luxury of pushing the replay button and reliving our lives. Mattie, confession is good for the soul, and I don't want some of these things charged to my account."

Chapter 17

A LOST PRIZE

We all have known people who have lost things and have wondered how they could be so careless. It is easy to judge others if it has never happened to us. I told Mattie a story about a boy whose parents lost him when they were on a trip. They had gone to a place where many people had gathered. After several days, they prepared to return home to where they lived. A large group of kinsfolk, acquaintances, children, and friends hastily and excitedly started for home. As night came at the end of the day, a chill visited the camp because a child was missing. Can any one of us imagine losing one of our children? We cannot fathom how such a careless thing could happen. After consultations and interrogations, the parents determined that the lost child could not be accounted for by anyone, and the inevitable took place. They began to retrace their route searching for the child. Three days came and went before they found him. He was safe and sound, sitting in a place with a group of respected teachers, listening, and asking them questions about life's most important things. His mother asked him why he had dealt with them in such a way. His father and his mother were in shock, and sorrow had gripped them as they had anticipated the worst. This loss could have been forever. "Mattie, before we are harsh to judge these two, we must know that God chose them to raise his Son (Luke 2:41-50)."

The experiences of life can be like a ride on a rollercoaster that begins with a slow ride to the top and ends with a terrifying ride to the bottom. None of us can guarantee that we can hold onto life's most prized possessions. The list of things that can escape our grasp is nearly endless. The loss of a job, the slipping away of one's health, the alienations of cherished family members, separation caused by feuds with friends, death that snatches away someone close to our heart, and other circumstances can cause dreams and ambitions to fade.

Devastating consequences often leave people broken and hurting. Lives can be altered and crushed. The changes can come as fast as turning on or off a light switch. Life often deals us a hand that we would choose not to play, serves a meal on a plate that we did not order, and summons us to witness things we did not want to see. I have stood with children who have lost their parents; I have consoled parents who have lost their children; I have wept with people who have lost their mates; and I have watched as friends were separated by death. Death is an appointment we all must keep. The old saying is true, "King or street sweeper, we all have to dance with the Grim Reaper."

If we had but one choice, what is the most prized possession we would most hate to lose? We should think before we answer because we have only one choice. This question leads us into deep water, provokes deep thought, and invites a long look at things we value most. We should ask ourselves, "What is that one thing I value most that I would not be willing to part with?"

Many people facing this decision and making this choice may resort to some drastic measures. To escape these gut-wrenching and heartbreaking choices, a person will bargain, bribe, barter, beg, and even try to buy his way out.

Because I am a pilot, I have had multitudes of people choose to fly with me throughout the years. Some of these passengers were on their first ride, and some had ridden several times. Some were old, and some were young. The common thread that seemed to join them all was that none were willing to die. Aerobatics in a twin-engine airplane can cause a deathly quiet to come over all passengers, and I have witnessed passengers become deathly ill on some occasions. I have heard them confessing, praying, crying, and promising money if they could just get their feet on the ground. I installed a small red button on the dash on the passenger side panel of my airplane, a Beechcraft Duchess N-6720T. The label under it read "Panic Button." At my own expense, I placed this button solely to satisfy my passengers, and it became the source of many laughs on trips I took with others. It was a conversation piece, and it was the most noted piece of equipment I ever installed. It simply said:

PANIC BUTTON
PUSH IN CASE OF EMERGENCY

If people were fish, we could catch most of them on the first cast. Passengers would inquire about this red button and its purpose. Some people threatened to push it, and others chose not to touch it even if I said it was okay. Everyone on board showed the utmost respect for this button and treated it as though it were a bomb. I told so many stories about this button that I was afraid someone might burn me at the stake if they learned the real truth. I wondered if the man who bought my airplane let his curiosity cause him to push that button, but I did not hear the noise.

Life has a way of robbing us of some of life's most prized possessions. The distress, the despair, the decisions, and the danger associated with any loss may make us want to push the panic button. The stress of the moment can paralyze us and render us helpless. The path of faith should be the easiest to follow, but sometimes it is the hardest to find because it is the least traveled. God often sends guides to those who are searching for the way, often someone who knows the way. No one I know sits around worrying about the things we might lose. Would a woman refuse to wear a beautiful diamond given to her by her sweetheart for fear that she might lose it? She would wear this priceless gift with such sentimental value as an expression of love and affection even though there was a possibility of losing it. Yet things that are precious and priceless can be lost.

A normal workday at the water company that I run is never predictable. It can be like a lamb or an alligator in that we can be petting it one minute and it can be eating us the next. One telephone call can change the complexion of things before we can blink our eyes. One minute we were swimming downstream; then the phone rang. Suddenly we began swimming upstream looking for a water leak. I recall one day when Mattie, Russell Barefield, and I got into the truck to go to the vicinity of Baskin, Louisiana. Our first stop was at the bridge over Looney Canal on the Seymore Road. We walked on each side of the bridge, but we observed no leak. Our next stop to look at ditches that were dry was at the intersection of Louisiana State Highway 857 and the Company Farm Road. The hunt then took us to the Roger Miller Road where we found a significant leak and spent time marking the site with blue flagging and paint. We placed a telephone call to Louisiana One Call so utilities would be located before the repair.

A four-mile trip brought us to the intersection of Louisiana Highway 15 and Parker Lane. Turning west onto Parker Lane, I looked to see where Mattie was lying. I was shocked when she was not in her usual places. I panicked and threw open the doors. Russell and I looked under and behind the seats. Mattie was not there. With a lump in my throat and Russell thinking this may be his last ride, we started our search for her. The top speed for this slow company truck was only 102 miles per hour. At that point, I thought I could jog faster than this snail's pace. Back at the bridge on Seymore Road, we called for Mattie, but we left the site empty-handed. I would have swapped this truck plus a lot more to boot in exchange for a muscle car to get to the next site. The only time I thought I could make up some time was in the curves if I could keep the truck from fishtailing. Mattie was not at the Company Farm and Highway 857 intersection. Russell placed a two-handed grip on the handhold over the door. With me in a cold sweat, we headed for the Roger Miller Road where we had previously stopped. When we arrived at this place, a Franklin Parish Police Jury truck with a pothole patcher was working on the road at the exact spot where we had marked the leak. I stood on the running board of the truck and asked the driver if he had seen a little gray and black wire-haired dog. His reply nearly made me go goofy, and he got to see a grown man cry, as I feared that I would never see Mattie again. The noisy piece of equipment left, and my feathers fell. I spoke her name quietly toward heaven and called loudly for all on earth to hear. The echoes of her name flew in all directions as I wondered how I became so distracted that something like this could happen. If there were a panic button, I would have already pushed it.

From the direction of the pine thicket, I heard a sound coming like someone running on a road full of Rice Krispies — snap, crackle, and pop — coming straight at me through the weeds and grasses. Mattie looked like she had been shot out of a bazooka. Upon reaching the road ditch, she became airborne and jumped all the way across the road into my waiting arms. The prodigal son's father was no prouder to see his son than I was to see Mattie. There was a celebration in the middle of the road as I danced a jig, and Russell danced a jig because he was still shaking a leg from the ride. Mattie must have thought I was a lollipop because she licked me all over and stuck to me like glue the rest of the day.

Mattie lay so close to me that night that I knew she wondered if I had left her on purpose. She had got out of the truck only to be close to me, and I failed to notice that she was not with us when we left. As I pulled away, she must have remembered someone else who threw her away and never came back. The approaching noise from the pothole patcher and her fear forced her to flee to another thicket. This time it was different because she recognized the voice of someone who loved her calling to her.

We learn many lessons in life from our experiences. Sometimes we spend all of our lives trying to decide what is important and what is unimportant. This exercise helps people sort out the things they value most. "Mattie Grace, most people I know put thinking about these things on the back burner. They may warm them up from time to time, but they don't finish and eat the meal. Indigestion is often the result of a lack of digestion. Mattie, yesterday helped me today to think about tomorrow. When I lost you and thought I may never see you again, I began to take inventory of things I value most." The one thing I learned is that my value system has changed dramatically throughout my life.

"Mattie Grace, let's get down to where the rubber meets the road and see if we can arrive at some conclusion about this question. What is that one thing I value most that I would not be willing to part with? Mattie, this is deep water that provokes deep thought as I wrestle to know the wishes of my own heart." I have known people who were motivated and driven to possess things they thought would satisfy their desires. As these things came into their possession, their appetite and hunger for more continued. Their cry for more never ended. When we look at people like this, the sad thing is that they may appear to be rich on the outside but may actually be bankrupt on the inside. This path looks familiar to me because I have traveled this way before. The path looks a lot different when I look back to where I have been rather than toward the sunset where I am going. I have picked up a lot of things and brought them along on my journey only to realize as I get closer to the end that I do not need them anyway. Instead of these things helping me, they may have hindered me.

One day Mattie Grace and I sat on the west bank of Lower Lake, a tranquil woods lake, soaking up the splendor of another sunset. The tracks I first made here as a boy had long since faded, but the memories had not. I remembered when we camped here climbing up into an elm tree and throwing the moss down, then picking the sticks out of it for Buck, the American Saddle Horse, to eat. In the springtime, the wildflowers decorated the landscape in a myriad of colors. Then I thought of home, the one I had left and the one I am going to. I had filled the closets at the tin-top house with a lot of things accumulated on my journey. These were things I wanted and thought I had to have. As I thought about the rest of the journey and the Big House, I found something I almost missed. It was a truth that was nearly hidden, a kind of delusion that obscured its discovery. Matthew 16:26 says, "For what is a man profited, if he shall gain the whole world, and lose his own soul? Or what shall a man give in exchange for his soul?" We must never let the things of the world hinder our trip to the Big House. Things temporal should never obstruct the view of the eternal.

"Mattie Grace, it is a matter of grace when men learn the truth that a man who has nothing can possess everything. Mattie, I think there are many, many people who live their lives and never learn this truth. It seems that all their energy and ambition is spent in possessing everything, and in the end they have nothing. A good start

170

ends in a sad finish. Life is like a baseball game that some enter in the top of the first inning and some in the bottom of the ninth. Some never enter the game. I never met a man who thought he entered the game too early, but I have met a bunch of men who wished they had entered it sooner."

I am an old man nearing the end of the journey. The truth that I learned is that I do not need the suitcase I packed a long time ago. I do not need anything from over here to help me get over there. I just need to catch the bus. Now, what was that one thing that I did not want to part with?

Chapter 18

A TRIP TO THE BIG HOUSE

“**M**attie, time will turn a page in your life, and if you are not careful, you can lose your place like in reading a book.” The journey for me started a long time ago, and there is a lot more road behind me now than there is in front of me. I have opened and closed a lot of doors, blown out a lot of candles, worn out a lot of boots and shoes, finished a lot of races, and counted a lot of sunsets. This has been a most enjoyable journey, and as the road grows shorter, I think much more about the destination. Like Abraham, I too look for a city “which hath foundations whose builder and maker is God (Hebrews 11:10).” I tell the mailman that if he brings my mail and I am no longer here, I have gone to the Big House. Please send my mail there because the Internal Revenue Service would be waiting for my reply.

The debate between the faith bunch and the not-of-faith crowd has always seemed a bit ridiculous to me. I find it very hard to believe that anyone would be absent of faith. The atheist or agnostic may have a dilemma if he holds to the position that he has no faith. Let me pose an example. A person may find it necessary to travel to a distant city. After buying airline tickets, he starts to board the flight. A total stranger, a man wearing a flight uniform with airman's wings on his lapel, meets him. This man introduces himself as the captain and says, “Welcome aboard.” What would we conclude about the traveler if he boarded the flight? Boarding the plane is either an act of faith or the action of a fool. This man in an airline uniform may be an impostor who could have bought his airman's wings from some toy store and who may never have taken one flight lesson. Each of us makes decisions each day to proceed based on the evidence and information at our disposal. These are acts of faith. If he does not believe what he observes, rejects all the evidence, and still boards the flight, he is a fool.

A non-believing pilot friend of mine and I had many discussions about arriving at the final destination at the Big House. I had hoped that one day he would find his way there. He had a copy of the approach plates in the King James Version that I gave to him for his flight to the Big House. All of us who fly instruments, not by the seat of our pants, have had to rely on instrument approach plates to arrive at a particular destination. While we may have never flown to this place before and we cannot see the destination with our eyes because of bad weather, we are assured that our flight will land safely if we follow the instructions on the instrument approach charts and obey the instrument flight rules. Deviating from these instructions could be fatal, and only a fool would try. I suggested to my friend to practice his not-of-faith position on his next flight. I told him to throw away the published IFR charts and draw a set of his own. Then he could take his chances of arriving safely at some destination. I will not be with him on the flight when he tests his charts. His confidence that he is right does not impress me. The designer of the airport has published the necessary charts to guarantee a safe arrival, and the Designer of the Big House sent us the Scriptures to show us how to get there. I tell Mattie Grace, "Don't get on the bus if the driver doesn't know where he is going."

The philosophical arguments for the existence of God and the intellectual exercises needed to arrive at a logical and rational conclusion no longer interest me. I matriculated in academic circles, discussing the ontological, teleological, cosmological, first cause argument, argument by design, and all the other theories. Trying to reach a conclusion was like riding a merry-go-round. I paid a little money, spent a lot of time, saw the same scenery, heard the same ole song, and got off at the same place where I got on. After all of this study and debate, I emphatically state that "I believe" and that my decision was not simply a leap in the dark. The acid baths of skepticism have been trying to wash away the truth all of my life. The foundation for faith grows firmer for me as my journey continues. DNA evidence and genetic profiling can support the declaration of the scientific community that man came from a common ancestor. Just as my journey began from the earth, I will return to the place of my beginning. I have a deep kinship with the earth since I am a part of it, and I welcome my return to it. He is the Potter, and I am the clay.

As I look back over the tailgate, I wonder how time slipped by so quickly. It seems that I have lived ten lives in one lifetime. The trip has been fast and furious. However, as I think about tomorrow, I know that the mountains are getting higher, the road is getting longer, time is getting shorter, and the stop sign may be just around the next curve. All the money in the world could not buy the experiences and treasures that have blessed my life, for these things have made me a wealthy man. Life for me has been a lot like a gumbo with many ingredients, flavors, and seasonings that have contributed to its uniqueness. My son referred to me as a dirt farmer; acquaintances referred to me as a daredevil crop duster and airline transport pilot; teachers referred to me as a student who never set the curve but had a hunger to learn; and others referred to me as a honky-tonk musician. I have been a roughneck, driller, and geologist in the oil patch and a certified water operator who wet many whistles. Colleagues said I was a preacher who needed a lot of polish. A host of folks thought I could qualify for a crazy check. My ticket to the Big House does not depend on what people think of me, and it is not by popular vote. My trip will not be decided by a committee that can determine my fate and destiny. My case is in the hands of One I completely trust to plead my cause, and it is my understanding that He has never lost a case, not even one. An interruption of the journey can come swiftly and unexpectedly for any of us.

As soon as I heard Mary Ann scream my name, I knew something bad had happened. Urgency and frantic sounds of panic filled the house. Every creature inside and outside was alerted and knew that something or someone unwanted had come to visit us. A scene I wish I could erase stood before my eyes. Mary Ann was standing at the top of the stairs cradling a ball of fur in her arms and crying that Mattie had just been killed by a truck. I completely lost it as the pain and hurt invaded me from the tips of my toes to the top of my head, and I wished it had been me and not her. I loved this little ole special needs dog more than I could ever describe. The feeling of sorrow permeated this whole household, and the expression of disbelief was reflected in every face because our family had been robbed of a very precious member. I took her in my arms and strained to look through a river of tears for any sign of life—a breath, a felt heart-beat, and a hope that never came. I sat on the floor in the great room as each member of our family, all the cats and dogs, filed by to say goodbye to Mattie. Each one grieved in his own way. Some cried out to her, some stood in silence as they looked at her, and others lingered longer in my lap next to her. With her lifeless body cradled in my arms, I slowly arose and walked through the front doors to share our loss with the Rest of the Gang. I left the doors open so that those inside could go with us on this walk. The chickens came run-ning from all directions and formed a solemn assembly. The guineas gathered in total silence in an uncharacteristic display of reverence, and the mules and the horse Cinnamon stood at attention as the pres-ence of sadness gripped us all.

I walked around and around and around the house, back to the barn, and back again. The host that followed us reminded me of the funeral dirges seen in the streets of New Orleans as they send off one of their own. As we went by the four Martin houses, I knew that Mattie would not be here to see them when they returned in the spring. I wondered if some of them would find their way to the Big House. This mystery of migration, threaded through much of creation, is a fascinating exercise that is awesome—a God Thing. I walked with Mattie on her last visit with the Rest of the Gang, those who lived outside: the chickens, guineas, the mules, the horse, Little Man, and Little Hen.

Someone standing at Mattie Grace's grave today and looking to the east could climb the steps to the front porch and walk through double doors to stand in the great room sixty yards away. There will always be a big empty space in this house that was left behind when Mattie moved to the Big House. She was like a little dynamo, and her motor was always running. The lights seemed to burn brighter and the sounds of excitement bounced off the walls. The first time I stood in this place and held her in my arms, I promised to love her as if she were my child. I vowed that the abuse and suffering she had endured would never happen to her again while she was in my care.

I watched a fabulous transformation take place as I put Mattie on the floor the first time and told her to look around to see what she thought. Those ears that drooped sadly so close to her face began to fly like flags at half-mast. Her tail seemed to wag the whole dog. Her eyes that had been filled with sadness began to flicker with flames of faith in a new way of life. I watched a heart nearly empty of hope begin to draw from a well of healing from the outside in and from the inside out. Mercy had given birth to a miracle. I told Mattie, "I want you to enjoy your stay here. We will run and play and have big fun everyday."

Mattie Grace was the spark plug of our family, and things would never be the same. I brought her to the front porch and sat on the south end with my back against the brick pillars. Mary Ann came to join me, along with Wiggles, Meg, Scooter, and the two ratters, Boo and Bach. Wiggles expressed her loss through low whimpering cries as though she were trying to get Mattie to come run and play, their bond broken by death. Mary Ann took these members of our family into the house and left me alone to say goodbye to Mattie. Cutting my heart out would have been less painful because I loved her so much. Just minutes earlier, she had seen a pecan bandit, a red fox squirrel, as he crossed the road next to the river. The tree stands next to the driveway by the blacktop road, and its pecans are inviting to the squirrels that nest in the thicket by the river. The passion for the chase ended Mattie's life instantaneously as a speeding truck struck her in her pursuit of the thief. Mary Ann's calls for help alerted every creature on the farm as she ran from the road with Mattie in her arms. What she had witnessed broke her heart.

As I sat holding Mattie, I looked into those big brown eyes. It was as though she were focused on some intriguing sight; it must have been the Big House. I did not want to let her go; I was not ready to say goodbye; I needed to hold her a little longer. This moment reminded me of something that happened nearly twenty-five years ago.

I have flown many sick children and their parents to St. Jude Children's Hospital in Memphis, Tennessee, for medical treatment. Families find a community of love and support there where care and concern are hallmarks of the place. On one trip there I sat in the waiting room waiting to carry a young patient and her mother home from the final treatment for cancer. Completing life's circle, this young girl is now a mother, and she came by my office one month ago to show me her first child.

While I waited for my passengers, another young mother came and sat next to me. Her nine-year-old daughter, who was deathly sick from her chemotherapy treatment, was with her. This young patient was waiting for a specific amount of time after treatment before being discharged. The child begged for a drink of water from the fountain just fifteen feet away. The mother placed the child on the bench, and her fight with cancer ended before her mother returned. The possibility of losing this fight had not prepared this broken-hearted woman for this moment. Sobbing, crying and completely broken, the mother picked her child up in her arms and rocked her back and forth calling her name over and over and over again. The staff and doctors tried desperately to get her to give the child up. Her refusal and pleas to let her hold her baby just a little longer, just a little longer, just a little longer brought a host of people who bathed this waiting room in tears. I adjourned to a flowerbed on the outside of the building, knelt behind a row of shrubbery, and watered them with my tears.

As I held Mattie in my arms that day, I rubbed her tummy and took my fingers to gently close those beautiful brown eyes. My tears stained the porch of the tin-topped house. I wish Mattie could tell me if she enjoyed her stay here. Part of an old man died with her.

As I dug her grave, I was not sure if she needed me or if I needed her more, but I knew this match was destined to be. Her presence in my life made me a better person. The lessons I learned from Mattie about grace are often missing in Sunday school literature. I wrapped her in a large bath towel, placed her in a small box, and buried her facing to the east toward the house. Mary Ann and I buried a part of us with her. This body was not a mere mass of protoplasm to be thrown away and discarded in a trash pile like her mother and her brothers and sisters. The best things in life are often found in the most unlikely of places. Her grave will always be a reminder that none of us will live here in the tin-top house forever. Mattie Grace is now forever at the Big House.

The sting of tragedy and death has been a plague of the human race and creation, a crisis that is never ending and is as old as life itself. Death is no respecter of persons, and we are never prepared when it summons someone from the ranks of our friends, family, the young and the old, strangers or acquaintances. Forty-six years ago, I stood under an old cedar tree in our local cemetery as the grave keepers covered the grave of one of my dear friends. I walked there to be alone as I wept for his wife and kids whose hurt was evident in their faces. Our friendship began as we started school together, and tears flowed freely as I embraced these memories. Suddenly a hand on my shoulder startled me. The man touching me was an old preacher, more seasoned and much more experienced than I was. He looked at me and said, "Son, it will get easier as you go along." There must be something terribly wrong with me because conducting funerals has never been easy, and the fear of failing families at a time of their greatest need burdens me. Our best is not good enough to soothe the pain of sorrow. If dealing with death is going to get easier, I want to know when.

The trips to the places of the habitation of the dead are becoming much too frequent. Tomorrow I will stand just beyond the old cedar tree on the hill. This funeral to celebrate the life of another dear friend will be the one thousand and fifth service I have conducted in the past forty-six years. All the family will have as they leave the cemetery will be memories of their loved one and the promises from the One who loves them that death is not the end. The cedar tree will expect my visit once again, but the old preacher will not be there to tell me when it will get any easier. He has been gone a long time.

The last three years have had an enormous impact on this old man's life. Some decisions we make in life can make us vulnerable to pain, sorrow, hurt, and heartache. Little did I know that the things we love the most can make us hurt the most. I took Mattie in as an orphan and adopted her as though she were my child. I vowed that the pain, suffering, and abuse she endured as a pup would never happen to her again while she was in my care. I wanted her to enjoy her stay and have fun while at the tin-top house. Mattie was just a tiny package crammed to overflowing with energy, enthusiasm, excitement, curiosity, charm, and charisma. She scattered love around everywhere, the way the wind scatters leaves. Every day with her was an adventure with something new around every curve and over every hill. We made a stroll down the memory lane of my lifetime. This journey was what I meant when I said, "I will live yesterday again, as I teach her today, what I learned then." We lived a lot of yesterdays over again.

As I laid her body to rest in front of the tin-top house, a solemn sadness swept over all of our family. This day was one none of us would forget. I buried a part of me with her that day. Then I began to think about the rest of me, the leftovers of an old man who is getting closer to the end of the journey. I have told my wishes about my death and burial to many witnesses. I would like to die like Mattie Grace with my boots on and running wide open with my ears lying back on my neck like a rabbit. When I have made my last track, bury me in a grave three feet wide, six feet deep, eight feet long, and six feet south of where I buried Mattie. This body has served me well. It has taken a lot better care of me than I have taken of it, and I now will what is left of it back to the dust. Do not poison my remains with embalming fluids that will only pollute the earth. Wrap me in five white cotton sheets, and bury me quickly. Others should honor my request that my funeral should be a travel back in time, a simple, private and final act without fanfare. My suitcase has been packed a long time for my trip to the Big House. The absence or presence of some people or some things after my death will not have one thing to do with the final outcome. I need no preacher, for my life will speak whether good or bad. I need no funeral director, for if Jesus' friends could bury him, so can mine. I need no flowers, for they will wilt; feed a hungry person instead. I need no songs, for the birds will sing my melodies. I need no headstone, for real epitaphs are etched into the heart.

The trend in recent years has been to change our focus from life's simple things to indulge our egos in out-performing our friends with elaborate burials. Funerals are often like a circus, a three ring one at that. Everybody gets in on the act with bells and whistles, balloons and flowers, limousines and coaches, lights and veils, chauffeurs, attendants, directors, and the rest of the cast necessary for this paid production. Those running the show say the charges are necessary to feed the elephants. Instead of worrying about what has perished, we need to worry about rescuing the perishing.

We only live once, but if we do it right, once is enough. Many of us may alter some of the routes, roads, or detours we have taken, but we would not change the destination. Often we have been moved, awed, inspired, satisfied, and left breathless by a beautiful sunset, one so gorgeous that there are no words to describe it. The pastels, the colors, the hues, the lighting all blended in such a way that it will take the breath away. Are we witnesses to a God Thing? A young dog took an old man back in time. We visited places and dug up memories of a lot of yesterdays. The lessons we learn today help us prepare for tomorrow. As I stood and looked at one of these sunsets that would make anyone's cup run over, I picked Mattie up in my arms and told her to live everyday as though tomorrow may never come. I told her that this sunset reminded me that I did not have many more to count, but we would have fun and run and play every day.

Mattie and I shared a lot of sandwiches together that were all better than a Happy Meal at McDonalds. I packed many lunches, took her many places, taught her many lessons, and introduced her to many people. I was inspired by her life. I loved her so very much. No better companion could have helped me enjoy the memories of my life. Memories of her will always be etched in my heart. The headstone on her grave reads:

Mattie Grace
Came from a Thicket on the River
To live in this house
Now forever at the Big House

Someone may think that all I have are the yesterdays with Mattie, but, as my sun sets, the tomorrows at the Big House are on my mind. This story about an old man and a young dog that beat him to the Big House is "A Matter of Grace" story.

EPILOGUE

I took Mattie in as an orphan and adopted her as though she were my child. I vowed that the pain, suffering, and abuse she endured as a pup would never happen to her again while she was in my care.

Treasures like Mattie are found in the most unlikely of places. She stepped right out of a trash pile and right into my heart. This little junkyard dog brought so much joy to this old man's life.

Have you ever thought that there may be a treasure somewhere that could step into your life? It may be out of a pile of trash, an animal shelter, or one homeless wandering along a road. Some by chance may find you, but I would hope that you would rather go find them. May your treasure hunt, as "A Matter of Grace," be blessed.

PICTURES

Mattie, after 45 days of treatment

The Tin-Top House: The Home of All the Characters

All the Cats

Row 1-Buttons, Sweetie, Jake;
Row 2-BooBoo, Bach, Tipper;
Row 3-Patches, Muffin, and Scooter

Little Man, The Alarm Clock

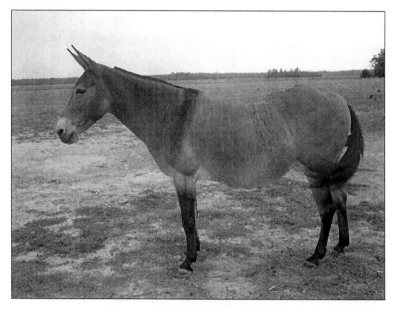

Willie, The Rambling Wreck

Lucy

Tensas and Cinnamon

Copper

Tensas

Chickens and Guineas

The Red Limousine: Wiggles When She Walks

Meg, the Sumo Wrestler

Drawing of Mattie, Our Trip to Colorado

Mattie's Headstone and Epitaph

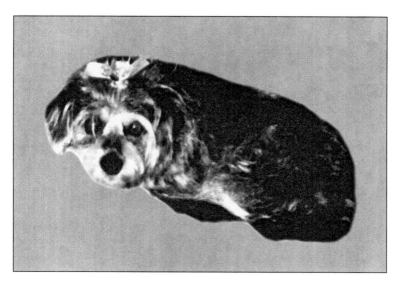

Groomed As If She Were Royalty

ABOUT THE AUTHOR

People who know Marion Collier say that he has lived his life fast and furious, as though he has lived ten lives in one lifetime. He has walked many paths—woodsman, survivalist, athlete, honky-tonk musician, crop-duster, oil field worker, skilled marksman, farmer, preacher, water manager, carpenter, animal lover, and storyteller extraordinaire. Over the last forty-five years, he has spoken to thousands of people as a preacher, teacher, entertainer, and motivator. He has served at the heart of his community in North Louisiana and has many colorful stories to tell. His journey with Mattie Grace began when she walked out of a trash pile and into his heart, inspiring him to write this story. He lives on his farm near Crowville, Louisiana, with his wife Mary Ann, seven mules, one horse, nine cats, three dogs, over two hundred fowl, and his pet rooster, Little Man.

From his lifetime of experiences in the Tensas Swamp, Marion learned basic life skills as a naturalist, outdoorsman, and sur-vivalist. The woods, the rivers, and the lakes were great training grounds for him. He is a member of the National Rifle Association, a Charter Member of the National Wild Turkey Federation, a pre-vious Louisiana State Turkey Calling Champion, and a competitive shooter in Black Powder Cartridge Silhouette, American Rimfire Association, BR-50, and skeet. He has been an avid gun collector since he was a young boy, and his walls are decorated with many fine and unusual pieces.

Aviation has been a part of his life for over forty years. His rat-ings include Airline Transport Pilot and Certified Flight Instructor and Multi-Engine Instruments. As owner of Collier Flying Service, he flew as a crop duster for twenty-five years. He has logged more than 30,000 hours, many with flight students, many with medical patients, and many who tell unforgettable tales about their first rides with him.

Marion is a graduate of Crowville High School. He attended Northeast Louisiana University, graduated from Mississippi College, and holds a Master's Degree in Theology from New Orleans Baptist Theological Seminary.

Currently he is the Systems Manager for North Franklin Water Works, Inc. He is a certified water operator and holds Class IV ratings in water production, distribution, and treatment. He was voted Louisiana Operator of the Year by the Louisiana Rural Water Association.

CPSIA information can be obtained at www.ICGtesting.com
Printed in the USA
LVOW090451291111

256825LV00001B/5/P